Ensuring Network Security through the Use of the Honeypot Technique

Ensuring Network Security through the Use of the Honeypot Technique

By

Rajalakshmi Selvaraj
and Kuthadi Venu Madhav

Cambridge Scholars Publishing

Ensuring Network Security through the Use of the Honeypot Technique

By Rajalakshmi Selvaraj and Kuthadi Venu Madhav

This book first published 2020

Cambridge Scholars Publishing

Lady Stephenson Library, Newcastle upon Tyne, NE6 2PA, UK

British Library Cataloguing in Publication Data
A catalogue record for this book is available from the British Library

ISBN (10): 1-5275-4143-6
ISBN (13): 978-1-5275-4143-6

Table of Contents

CHAPTER 1 1
INTRODUCTION

1.1 BACKGROUND 1
1.2 PROBLEM STATEMENT 11
1.3 OBJECTIVES OF THE STUDY 14
1.4 JUSTIFICATION 17
1.5 OUTLINE OF THE BOOK 18

CHAPTER 2 19
LITERATURE REVIEW

2.1 INTRODUCTION 19
2.2 ANOMALY BASED INTRUSION DETECTION SYSTEM 20
2.3 DISTRIBUTED APPROACH FOR IDS 22
2.4 TRUST BASED IDS 25
2.5 CLUSTER AND GROUP BASED IDS 27
2.6 INTELLIGENT IDS 28
2.7 IDS IN MANET 29
2.8 IDS FOR HETROGENEOUS WSN 30
2.9 ENTERTAINMENT THEORETIC APPROACH FOR ID 31
2.10 IDS FOR VARIOUS ATTACKS 32
2.11 AGENT BASED IDS 33
2.12 TRAFFIC ANALYSIS BASED INTRUSION DETECTION 34
2.13 IMMUNITY BASED IDS 35
2.14 OPTIMIZED ALGORITHMS USED FOR ID 36
2.15 DATA MINING APPROACH FOR IDS 37
2.16 ENERGY EFFICIENT IDS 38
2.17 CONCLUSION 41

CHAPTER 3 42
MOTIVATION

3.1 HONEYPOT: INTRUSION IDENTIFICATION TECHNIQUE....... 42
3.2. ANT-BASED DDoS TECHNIQUE UTILIZING ROAMING VIRTUAL HONEYPOTS 43
3.3 EIDS BASED HONEYPOT SYSTEM 43
3.4 EIDPS: AN EFFICIENT APPROACH T0 PROTECT THE NETWORK AND INTRUSION PREVENTION 44
3.5. AN EFFIDIENT ODAIDS-HPS MECHANISM FOR RESPONDING PREVENTING AND DETECTING THE DDoS ATTACKS 45

CHAPTER 4 47
HONEYPOT TECHNIQUE FOR INTRUSION DETECTION

4.1 INTRODUCTION TO INTRUSION DETECTION 47
4.2 NECESSITY OF INTRUSION DETECTION SYSTEMS 48
4.3 OVERVIEW OF PROPOSED WORK 48
4.4 INTRUSION DETECTION 49
4.5 HONEYPOT.......... 51
4.6 PACKETS ANALYSIS.......... 53
4.7 SUPPORT VECTOR MACHINE 54
4.8 IDS ALGORITHM.......... 55
4.9 RESULTS AND DISCUSSION.......... 57
4.10 CONCLUSION 64

CHAPTER 5 65
DDoS DETECTION BASED ON THE ANT TECHNIQUE USING ROAMINGVIRTUALHONEYPOTS

5.1 INTRODUCTION.......... 65
5.2 ROLE OF HONEYPOT IN THE DETECTION OF DDoS ATTACK.......... 69
5.3 PROPOSED SOLUTION.......... 70
5.4 SIMULATION RESULTS 79
5.5 CONCLUSION 86

CHAPTER 6 87
ENHANCED INTRUSION DETECTION SYSTEM PERFORMANCE USING FIRECOL PROTECTION SERVICES BASED HONEYPOT SYSTEM

6.1 INTRODUCTION 87
6.2 PROPOSED WORK 88
6.3 DEPLOYMENT CLASSIFICATION 92
6.4 RESULTS AND DISCUSSION 93
6.5 CONCLUSION 104

CHAPTER 7 105
EIPDS: AN EFFECTIVE TECHNIQUE TO SECURE THE NETWORK FROM INTRUSION

7.1 INTRODUCTION 105
7.2 MOTIVATION 107
7.3 INTRUSION DETECTION SYSTEMS 107
7.4 IDPS (INTRUSION DETECTION AND PREVENTION SYSTEMS COMPONENTS 111
7.5 OVERVIEW 113
7.6 RESULTS AND DISCUSSION 119
7.7 SUMMARY 122

CHAPTER 8 123
AN EFFECTIVE ODAIDS-HPS APPROACH FOR PREVENTING, DETECTING AND RESPONDING TO DDoS ATTACKS

8.1 INTRODUCTION 123
8.2 DENIAL OF SERVICE 124
8.3 MOTIVATION 125
8.4 TYPES OF DDoS ASSULTS 125
8.5 DDoS ATTACK OVERVIEW 127
8.6 INTERNET ARCHITECTURE OF DDoS 128
8.7 OVERVIEW 130
8.8 RESULTS AND DISCUSSION 134
8.9 SUMMARY 139

CHAPTER 9 140
CONCLUSIONS AND FUTURE WORK

REFERENCES 143

CHAPTER 1

INTRODUCTION

1. 1 BACKGROUND

A 'wireless sensor network' (WSN) is defined as a group of hubs sorted into a useful network. Every hub contains handling capacity and may contain numerous sorts of memory, have an RF handset, have a force source, and suit different sensors and actuators (Butun, Morgera and Sankar 2014). In the wake of being sent in a specially appointed manner, the hubs convey remotely and frequently self-sort out. WSNs have uncommon components in contrast with past remote systems, which had sensor hubs with lower quality, hub arrangements with denser levels and computation, restrictions of capacity (Liu and Yu 2008) and overwhelming vitality. These elements create more difficulties in the application and advancement of WSNs. These WSNs have been broadly utilized around the world in recent years.

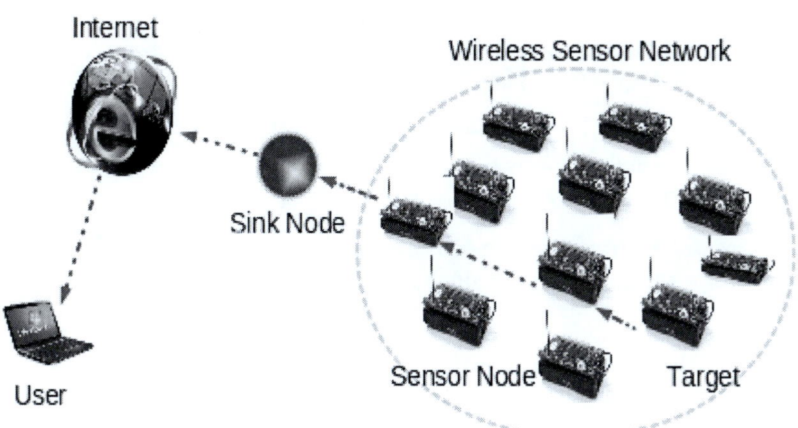

Figure 1.1 Basic structure of a wireless sensor network

Sensor hubs in a WSN perform in a territory of interest and work with less power, less cost and, furthermore, with few capacities. Despite the fact that the size of these sensor hubs is small, they are given radio handsets, sensors and implanted microchips. As can be seen from Figure 1.1 (Yu, Luo and Min 2010), sensor hubs transmit over a short separation by means of a remote medium and team up to fulfill a typical assignment that is then sent to the client through the sink hub, for instance, the control of a mechanical procedure, the observation of a front line, or the checking of an environment. Sensor systems have accompanying one-of-a-kind qualities and requirements in contrast to conventional remote correspondence systems, for instance, cell frameworks and MANET (Shen, Li, Xu and Cao 2011).

Dense node deployment: In a field of interest, sensor hubs are normally vigorously conveyed.

Power of sensor nodes: Batteries control the sensor hubs in a sensor system, so in certain circumstances it is hard to energize the batteries in a sensor system.

Calculation, basic vitality and capacity confinements: Sensor hubs in a sensor system are vigorously confined in their calculation, vitality and capacity ranges.

Setup: Sensor hubs in the sensor systems by and large perform haphazardly with no arrangement. They autonomously coordinate themselves in the event that they perform in a system.

Settled application: For a specific application, by and large, only the system is arranged and performed. The requirements of the outline of a system may change with its use.

Deceitful sensor nodes: In sensor systems, sensor hubs for the most part perform in the most exceedingly terrible situations and perform with no data. This causes disappointments for the sensor hubs.

Interminable change of topology: The topology of the system perpetually changes if there is hub disappointment.

Numerous-to-one traffic pattern: This activity example is exhibited in a few utilizations of sensor systems. In this activity, design information is spilled out of numerous sensor hubs to one particular sink.

Information redundancy: Sensor hubs in sensor systems are performed in an area of interest and take an interest in understanding a standard detection assignment in most sensor system applications. Consequently, the detected information in the sensor hubs has a clear level of excess.

With respect to the system and the arrangement of the system, the components of sensor systems and the requirements of different applications majorly affect the expectations of the system outline. The primary points of the system outline are delineated below.

Size of the tiny node: Among the points of the system outline, the reduction of the hub size is an essential one. Many sensor hubs in the sensor systems by and large perform in a most exceedingly terrible environment. Hub sending can be encouraged, and the force, utilization and expense of sensor hubs can additionally be diminished by decreasing the hub's size.

Minimal cost of the hub: The second vital point of the system outline is minimizing the hub's cost. Since numerous sensor hubs in the sensor systems by and large perform in a most exceedingly awful environment and the system cannot reuse those sensor hubs, it is fundamental to minimize the sensor hubs' cost so that the system expense is minimized.

Minimum consumption of power: A major and imperative point in the sensor system outline is reducing power utilization. Sensor hubs in the sensor systems are fueled by batteries and it is hard to revive the hubs, so the goal should be for the life span of the system and its sensor hubs to be drawn out.

Setup: Sensor hubs in the sensor systems for the most part perform with a range of energy with no arrangement. They coordinate themselves freely in the event that they perform in a system and, if there is a disappointment of the hubs, the topology of the system may change.

Versatility of the sensor organizers: The quantity of sensor hubs in the sensor system is adaptable so that the composed conventions for the system can be versatile enough to adapt to different system sizes.

Unwavering quality of the sensor systems: Data ought to be conveyed with no intrusion in the utilization of the sensor system. To convey this solid information with no intrusion, the planned protocols of the system ought to give blunder redress and control plans.

Deficiency sufferance: Disappointments of sensor hubs in the sensor system occur because of the noticeably bad surroundings and undesirable operations, so the goal is that they should be flaw tolerant.

Security: Sensor hubs in the sensor systems perform in a most exceedingly terrible environment and thus are prone to attacks, particularly in various military applications. In such circumstances, to shield a sensor hub from illicit access or the information/data in the sensor system from dangerous attacks, effective security plans must be presented.

Channel utilization of the sensor system: Due to its restricted transmission capacity, a sensor system's use of the channel gets diminished so that planned conventions can be presented for effective channel use.

QoS Support: Different utilizations of sensor systems may have different qualities of service (QoS) as far as bundle misfortune and idleness of conveyance in sensor systems are concerned.

1.1.1 WSN Intrusion Detection

An undesirable action in the system is called an 'intrusion'. Intrusion recognition is a noteworthy improvement and exploration theme that influences secrecy, accessibility and honesty. The Intrusion Detection System (IDS) runs in order to recognize undesirable intrusions for wired systems, thus it helps to accomplish a wide security method (Rao and Nayak 2014). To create an intrusion detection system for wired systems, there are distinctive methodologies and techniques, yet a few strategies are not practical for remote systems. Because of the varying quality of remote sensor organizers, the IDS made for wired systems is not appropriate for WSNs. The isolation of the dangerous, unordinary hub from the system is the real technique of the IDS in a WSN. An IDS actualized for a WSN is vital in order to find surprising, performing, not performing or damaging hubs (Li, Li, Fu and Ming 2010). Other vital perspectives for WSN security are physical security and remote transmission: above all, flagging and spying remote assault transmissions. The actualized intrusion location framework ought to evaluate the flagging and spying. Fundamental capabilities for an IDS in a WSN are physical security and distinguishing harmed hubs. This point affords the respectability of the information and directs it through the entire system safely (Li, Pandit, Katneni and Agrawal 2012).

1.1.2 Attacks on wireless sensor networks

Security assaults on wired systems are unique in relation to those on a WSN (Jabez and Muthukumar 2015). These varieties are produced using specific properties of a WSN. The vitality of a WSN is its real key, and its security includes classification, accessibility and uprightness parts. Elements of these security nuts and bolts are clarified below.

Classification: Confidentiality is the real component in the digital security worldview. At the base of this is the information transmitted in WSN systems. The information ought to be scrambled by the system to give it confidentiality. Encryption strategies such as symmetric and deviated ones can serve this encryption process. In contrast with symmetric encryption, deviated encryption is more grounded because of its private key methodology. WSN overseers ought to be certain about conveying their key when they utilize symmetric encryption. The overseer can be cautioned by a dependable and advantageous IDS about system security, or they can build up a safe key administration structure in their WSN.

Uprightness: Uprightness means information shielded from change by unapproved and undesired parties. Executives ought to be certain about uprightness to ensure their WSN is working appropriately. In a WSN, offering uprightness requires extra assets for calculation and creates additional bytes for sent information, so the engineering of the IDS can offer a noteworthy component of honesty.

Vitality: Sensors of WSNs have restricted computational assets and have constrained vitality. A WSN watches situations, and the life of the sensor is key to giving it additional time, and heads of WSNs avoid lessening the life of the battery of the sensor. Confronting this vitality approach is even more important for WSNs with regard to the parts of digital security administration. Some digital assaults are described below.

Denial of Service (DoS) Attacks: A major part of DoS assaults is to try to render an online administration inaccessible. Because of the qualities of WSNs, DoS assaults can be modified, and it is through the different qualities of WSNs that assailants give structure to their intrusions. Limited calculations and confined memory are frailties of WSNs, and these are exploited by gatecrashers. The equipment of the sensor hubs is another constraint of WSNs, and this is used by aggressors to benefit them. Assailants look to bring about WSN non-performances because of the way that WSNs work. The physical layer is a layer that can be influenced by other assaults. Sensors can be harmed because of the expansion of physical layer assaults.

Confusion: The steering data of WSNs can be changed by confusion assaults, and the entire WSN is adversely affected by these confusion assaults. The primary stage of this assault is to send the message back the wrong way. Some methodologies are described below to help us recognize confusion assaults.

- Utilizing hashed bundles of information results. Extra vitality is not required by this technique.
- Making and using a verification device between the transmitter and the recipient. This technique happens a great deal less in its execution.
- Utilization of secure multi-bounce steering. This strategy is not proficient enough to distinguish harmed hubs.

Specific Forwarding: Although harmed hubs act like a customary hub and send parcels, a few bundles are dropped in this sort of assault. In contrast with the dark opening/sinkhole assaults, specific forwarding is more grounded. The following gatherings are countermeasures for specific forwarding assaults:

- Detection in the light of acknowledgment.
- Detection with the utilization of the data of neighborhoods.
- Utilizing a multi-information stream to combat the assault.

Sinkhole Attack: In this sort of assault, a spurious hub is presented by an aggressor in the system. This spurious hub is utilized to launch an assault, which is called a sinkhole assault. Solicitations by the hubs for directions are observed by the aggressor. This assault's approach is targeted on the information join layer.

Sybil Attack: The Sybil assault is a harmed hub that performs the acknowledgment illegitimately. To acquire the expressed request in the WSN scientific categorization (Huang, Liao, Chung and Chen 2013), all hubs in the system need to perform with the assistance of different hubs. Harming this association is the principal point of this assault. The following are types of Sybil assaults:

- Indirect and direct correspondence
- Stolen characters and fabricated characters

- Non-synchronous and simultaneous assaults

A harmed hub can point hubs at the participation procedure, the routing convention and the component used for location with this assault.

Wormhole Attack: Without utilizing the system cryptographically, the system can be influenced by this assault on the WSN (Han, Jiang, Shen, Shu and Rodrigues 2013). Data are recorded at one harmed hub by an assailant, and the hub is then burrowed to some other area by the aggressor.

HELLO Flood Attacks: In a remote sensor system, in order to distinguish the closest hub for routing conventions, a few bundles called 'HELLO Parcels' are sent to the neighboring node. To polarize different sensors, this sort of digital assault utilizes bundles, particularly gatecrashers, as they have a substantial radio and handling force and can send HELLO parcels to a lot of sensors by squeezing an entire segment of the system. A sensor that gets parcels can expect the gatecrasher to be an ordinary hub.

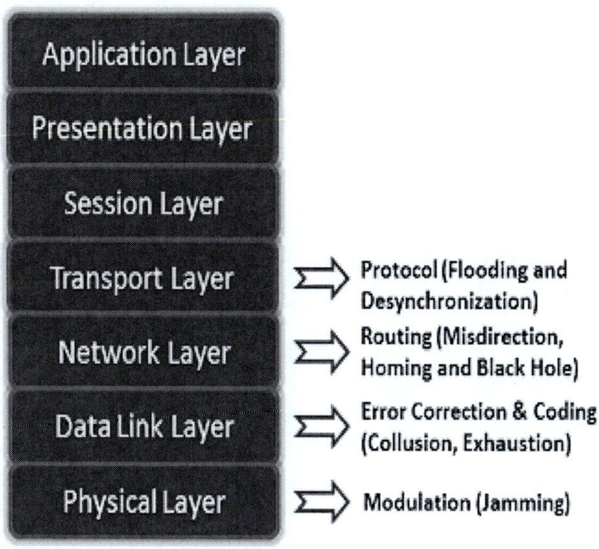

Figure 1.2. DoS Attack Types on WSN Layers (Muntjir, Rahul and Alhumyani 2017)

In Figure 1.2, DoS assaults will assault the physical layer of the WSN. Confusion assaults, specific forwarding assaults and sinkhole attacks appear as system layer assaults. Wormhole attacks will assault the data link layer of the WSN layer. High flood attacks will assault the transport layer of the WSN layer.

1.1.3 Classification of IDS for WSNs

In order to recognize internal or external digital assaults, the IDS can be characterized as programming or equipment devices that check the system. The objectives of the IDS are recognizing assaults, counteracting assaults by giving discouragement to the assailants, gathering proof from the system, serving situational mindfulness, and obtaining association policies (Coppolino, D'Antonio, Romano and Spagnuolo 2010). The IDS' design has four fundamental segments, which are the sensor, detector (analyze engine), knowledge base, and response component. In Figure 1.3, the sensor gathers information from the monitored system and the detector breaks down the gathered information to identify intrusions. The knowledge base serves to identify the marks of an assault and the response component deals with the reactions to assaults. As indicated by the screening activity, the procedure of the framework IDS is either named a 'Network-Based IDS' (NIDS) or a 'Host-Based IDS' (HIDS). A NIDS is on a circulated system and screens system activity to recognize intrusions that can be on this system. A HIDS is on a particular PC and screens the intrusions that can be on this machine. NIDS sensors can be in any part of a system. The consolidation of both a NIDS and a HIDS is named a 'Hybrid Framework'. In order to identify intrusions, there are two methodologies that are separated into two strategies, and are named 'anomaly detection' and 'misuse detection'.

Anomaly Detection: When a system exercises something that is unique in relation to typical framework practices, anomaly detection frameworks attempt to recognize that exercise. A few procedures of anomaly detection are portable specialist-based insights, data mining, and neural networks. In Figure 1.4, anomaly detection functions admirably for obscure assaults, however now and then its false ready rate can be high. The anomaly detection procedure gets reviewed information individually, looks at the information to choose whether there are any inconsistencies or not, and in the end, if there is any irregularity, it warns the framework with a reaction message (Dhakne and Chatur 2015).

Misuse Detection: This is a mark-based recognition. This strategy has a learning base, including marks of known assaults and feeble purposes of the framework. Misuse detection is extremely fruitful for identifying known assaults, however its downside is that it struggles to detect new obscure assaults.

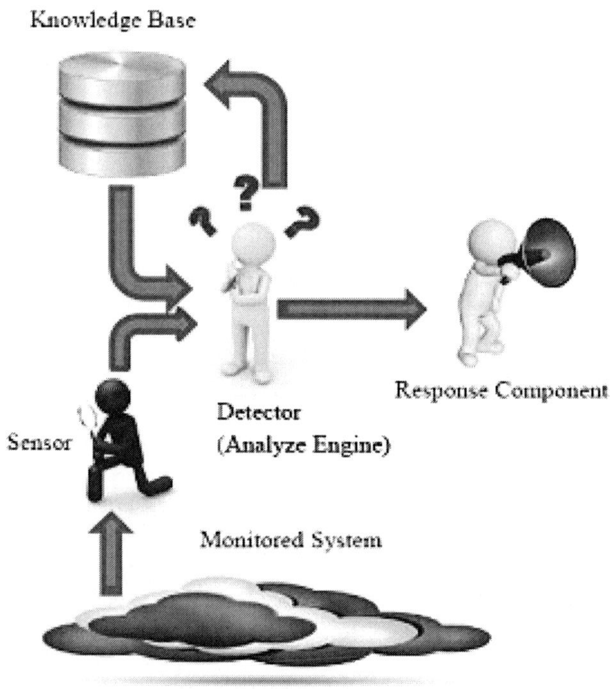

Figure 1.3. Basic structure of the IDS

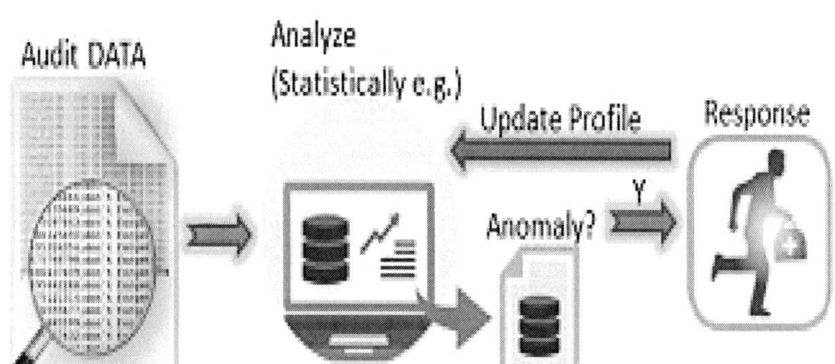

Figure 1.4. Structure of anomaly detection

1.1.4 IDS approaches in WSNs

Because of the structure of WSNs, security dangers happening in the remote sensor system are not quite the same as wired system dangers and limitations; it has, for example, a restricted battery life. A WSN has distinctive IDS approaches. All groupings of discovery methodologies made by various analysts happen from open IDS scientific classifications (misuse detection, anomaly detection). The order of methodologies is as follows: intrusion sort, interloper sort, discovery procedures, wellspring of the gathered information, investigating areas of the gathered information, utilization recurrence. The interloper sort is assembled into two classifications in a system. These classifications are inside interloper (narrow-minded or vindictive hub) and outer interloper (an outside assailant attempting to access the framework). The intrusion can be made by taking information, supplying false information and thus adjusting the framework, denying access to the framework, or affecting the vitality proficient as per the intrusion type in a WSN. A few papers also bring up cross-breed or determination-based discovery for location approaches. Fathinavid and Aghababa (2012) note that in determination-based recognition, security tenets are held to distinguish specific assaults and to examine hub practices. In the event that any circumstance occurs in which these rules are attacked, then the framework decides that there is an intrusion. The IDS methodology is isolated into two sections, which are unified IDS and conveyed IDS, as indicated by investigating areas of the gathered information.

Anomaly detection approaches in WSNs: Different types of anomalies are gathered as oddities of WSNs. Association issues existing in WSNs are portrayed by system peculiarities. Unusual and startling additions and removals are the data that show whether there is any intrusion or not. These signs are depicted as broadcast storms, episodic connectivity, a loss of connectivity, and routing loops. Equipment or programming issues on the sensors are called node anomalies. The disappointment of sun-based boards and power issues cause the signs of hub abnormalities. Jumbled information sets cause data anomalies in WSNs. These inconsistencies can be created from sensor or ecological issues. Different anomalies can be characterized as not fitting to another sort of oddity seen previously. These methodologies can be sorted as measurable-based, simulated insusceptible framework-based, machine learning-based, information mining-based and diversion hypothesis-based (El-Alfy and Al-Obeidat 2014).

WSN misuse detection methods: This is otherwise called signature-based IDS and is effective for recognizing known assaults (Yu and Tsai 2008).

The disadvantage of the misuse detection approach is that it cannot recognize new obscure assaults or assaults that do not have predefined rules. For WSNs, utilizing the misuse detection system is an unpredictable undertaking in light of the imitations of WSNs. For example, keeping indications of assaults is extremely troublesome and is not viable.

Hybrid detection approaches in WSNs: A hybrid methodology can be refined, like that which stays out of the anomaly and misuse recognition methods, or that which consolidates anomaly and misuse detection techniques (Sun, Shan, Wu and Xiao 2013).

1.2 PROBLEM STATEMENT

There are numerous existing research studies on intrusion detection in WSNs. Here we describe the disadvantages of existing systems.

Network Anomaly Detection & Intrusion Reporter (NADIR): At the Los Alamos National Laboratory, the NADIR was produced for use by the research facility in its internal PC security system. Therefore, with the issues and hierarchical needs of the Los Alamos National Laboratory in mind, the NADIR was imagined. It was not by any means planned as a widespread IDS. Data are gathered from three different types of administrative hubs, which is a truly tedious and progressive, continuous process.

Distributed Intrusion Detection System (DIDS): When utilizing DIDS, there are three principal segments: 1) a DIDS director, which is capable of breaking down all the information received from the two different segments and distinguishing conceivable assaults. The DIDS director investigates material from the host screens and the LAN screens that report to it and conveys the outcomes to the SSO; 2) a LAN screen, which screens all movement in a LAN section and reports unapproved or suspicious exercises in the system to the DIDS director; and 3) a succession of host monitors, in which the reviewed information is gathered and dissected. At that point it transmits the significant data to the DIDS director. Communications manager and framework manager are the two principal people reporting to the director. Information from the host screens and LAN screens is gathered by the communications manager and conveyed to the framework manager for further handling. Inductions about the security condition of the framework and every individual host are drawn by the framework manager. The framework manager gathers the data for presentation (Cárdenas, Berthier, Bobba, Huh, Jetcheva, Grochocki and Sanders 2014).

After an intrusion, it takes a very long time to advise the director through the screens, so it is an excessively protracted procedure, making it impossible to be a standard IDS. In a substantial system, it is exceptionally hard to keep constant contact between the screens as there can be such a large number of them. It is a various leveled procedure and a disappointment at any time may make the entire framework powerless.

Graph-Based Intrusion Detection System (GrIDS): In huge systems, in order to help with intrusion recognition, GrIDS prepares the creators by proposing a strategy for building diagrams of system action. Hosts on the systems are spoken to as hubs and associations between these hosts are spoken to as edges between these hubs in the diagram. In a substantial system, GrIDS is tedious and difficult to actualize. The framework director is completely detached from the discovery-based plan, in which the restorative activities are rendered unapproachable.

Co-Operating Security Managers (CSMs): CSMs have six segments: 1) a local intrusion detection component (IDS), which performs intrusion detection for the neighborhood host; 2) a security manager (SECMGR), which co-ordinates the conveyed recognition intrusion between CSMs; 3) an intruder handling part (IH), which takes action when an interloper is discovered; 4) a Graphical User Interface (GUI), which allows security heads to associate with individual CSMs; 5) a command monitor (CMNDMON), which catches the orders executed by clients and sends them to the IDS; and 6) a TCP communication (TCPCOM), which enables TCP correspondence between CSMs. An intrusion is only taken care of after the successful fulfillment of all six criteria, so CSMs are tedious. CSMs are not relevant for a quick review of vast quantities of information. On the off chance that the system size gets larger, it is difficult for CSMs to speak with the administrators.

Event Monitoring and Enabling Responses to Anomalous Live Disturbances (EMERALD): EMERALD has been proposed as a structure for adaptable and dispersed intrusion detection between operable PCs and a system. Internal aggressors are not identified by EMERALD, as it believes the hubs of the internal system (Cheng, Chi and Lau 2011). It requires message passing. It does not go for a high review investigation speed.

Autonomous Agents For Intrusion Detection (AAFID): The AAFID works with three parts: operators, handsets and screens. The framework is self-sufficient and requires no human specialist, yet at the same time it has a few issues. Screens are single purposes of disappointment in the AAFID control part. All the handsets that it controls stop delivering helpful data when a screen stops working. There are issues of consistency and duplication of data when copied screens are utilized, creating repetition. The AAFID design does not indicate access control components or take into account diverse clients having different levels of access to the IDS. The AAFID delays the recognition of intrusions at the screen level until all the fundamental data arrive from the specialists and handsets. This is an issue that is common to every single conveyed IDS.

Intrusion Detection and Rapid Action (INDRA): This utilizes a trusted system (Bao, Chen, Chang and Cho 2012) and creates alerts inside the system to advise about the suspected hosts. The biggest frailty of the framework is that INDRA needs trust, since intrusions may arise from any place, even from inside the trusted system. The likelihood of a false alert wins, which may put the entire framework in a precarious state. On the off chance that it originates from a trusted system, INDRA cannot adapt to the assault.

The following components should be considered in order to outline the proficiency of an IDS:

Time consumption: Additional time is required to recognize an intrusion more plausibly and make the interloper less effective, so a large and dependable IDS ought to be less protracted.

Multiple attack stability: Multiple intrusions are not liable to happen at the same time, but this scenario might still occur and none of these frameworks propose any system to handle numerous intrusions in this way.

Kind of reaction: The reaction can be either uninvolved or dynamic. The ideal path is to utilize a mixed reaction.

System association end: To identify or control an interloper, the use of an IDS appears to be very extreme, yet the best IDS ought not to require any sort of system association end.

Message spreading troubles: A decent IDS ought to be free from this issue in light of the fact that, at whatever point there is a need for a message to spread, there remains a chance of a false alert predicament.

Information handling: An IDS can incorporate or appropriate information handling. In any case, utilizing both can be far superior.

Trust issue: At each conceivable hub of the system, a perfect framework ought to be fit for recognizing intrusions. Altogether, a decent IDS should not utilize a trusted system.

A various leveled framework is not generally great: To work together with the lower level parts, a framework that has a progressive plan typically needs additional time. A novel IDS therefore ought to be variously leveled as little as could be expected under the circumstances.

The less reliance, the more productivity: There remains a possibility of a bottleneck when the segments of IDS are subject to each other. In the event that a solitary part falls flat, the entire framework may crumble. So there ought to be as little reliance as could be expected under the circumstances.

1.3 OBJECTIVES OF THE STUDY

The major aim is to determine how to detect attackers and hackers as well as how to gather information about the hackers. The captured data will be utilized for the upcoming investigations. We are proposing a novel concept known as a virtual honeypot, which will recognize and capture network intrusions.

Honeypot system

A honeypot is a data framework system set up as a decoy to distract hackers in order to gain access to information (Sokol, Husak and Liptak 2013). This definition incorporates two general concepts: 1) a honeypot can be any kind of PC asset because the expression data framework asset is extensively and purposefully characterized; and 2) a honeypot can be a work station, a gadget, a server or a whole system, and will be a distraction to capture an attacker. During the action performed by the attacker, sufficient information and data are extracted and verified. Honeypots can be utilized for generation or exploration reasons. A honeypot is also utilized for danger moderation generation. Most generation honeypots are imitations of particular working frameworks or administrations. As a result of assaults created via robotized instruments used to haphazardly search for and assume control of defenseless frameworks, systems and frameworks are secured by these honeypots. The checking procedure from these assault apparatuses can be backed right off by running a generation honeypot, squandering their time in this manner. Assaults can be closed and brought down by some generation honeypots, for instance, sending the aggressors an affirmation parcel with a window size of zero. At the point that the window size starts to build, the assault is put into a "hold" status in which it can just send information. Figure 1.5 demonstrates the engineering of the honeypot framework. The honeypots are open to the approaching aggressors as opposed to blocking them and occupy their attention with a false database instead of a genuine database and restrict the capacity of the assailants.

Figure 1.5 demonstrates the framework outline of the honeypot architecture. Firstly, a firewall protects the whole system. At that point, the whole framework is secured by a switch, and compartmented information layers are isolated from systems inside the association and outside clients or operating systems. An instrument called the honeynet secures the association system, which is a system of PCs' support in the honeypot design. IDSs are actualized in the framework for additional security and recognition. To deal with the logs made by the honeynet, a checking control framework is utilized. An observing control framework is additionally used to screen all the approaching sections in the system.

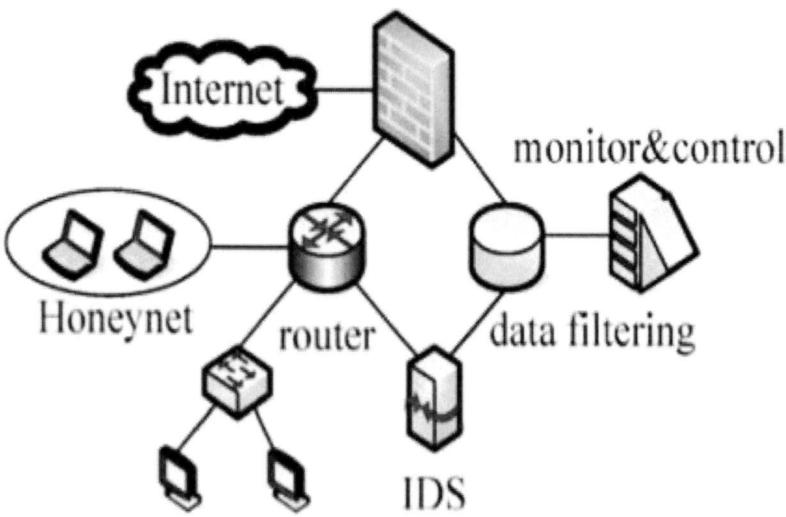

Figure 1.5. System design of honeypot architecture

1.3.1 Classification of Honeypots

Honeypots can be classified into two types.

Low-interaction honeypots: These are frequently utilized for generation purposes. As can be seen from Figure 1.5, low-interaction honeypots restrict their communication and work parameters by copying certain administrations and working frameworks. The honeypot constrains the assailant's exercises to the level of imitating.

Advantages:

1) Simple to set up and maintain.

2) The potential dangers are diminished by the restricted imitation permitted in low-interaction honeypots. In the case of low-interaction honeypots, it is a façade application that gives a bogus picture of an objective host. A façade assembles data about the assailant when it is tested or assaulted. As exteriors frequently require negligible establishment exertion and hardware, they offer basic, simple sending and can imitate an expansive assortment of frameworks.

***High-interaction honeypots**:* As high-interaction honeypots (Yu, Luo and Min 2010) include genuine working frameworks and applications, they are more mind-boggling. In the event that the aim is to gather data about hackers on a specific FTP server or administration, a genuine FTP server will be assembled. No limitations are placed on the aggressors' conduct as they are given genuine frameworks to connect with, and in order to catch broad insights about the full degree of a hacker's techniques, directors are permitted. To keep an attacker from further damaging data and servers, the honeypot framework itself, i.e. the system associated with the honeypot, should be separated in the worst-case scenario.

A characteristic of high-interaction honeypots is the conciliatory sheep, which is a framework purposefully left helpless against an assault. The honeypot will occasionally be inspected to figure out whether it has been traded off and, assuming that this is the case, what was done to it. A system sniffer placed close to the honeypot can gather extra information, for example, a point by point hint of charges sent to the honeypot. In any case, the honeypots themselves are "live" and in this manner introduce a conceivable bouncing off point for an aggressor. With the specific end goal of disengaging and controlling the honeypot, extra organization considerations must be made, for example, a method of firewalls or other system control technology, or the total separation of the honeypot from the internal system. All created outcomes are precisely as they would be for a genuine framework in light of the fact that conciliatory sheep are themselves genuine frameworks. Be that as it may, significant authoritative overheads, for example, the establishment of a fully working framework and a manual, are required by conciliatory sheep (Sokol, Husak and Liptak 2013).

The second characteristic of high-interaction honeypots is an authentic working framework that gives data, regulations and control. Here, proficient security engineers have altered the working framework and portion, not at all like the conciliatory sheep model. The qualities of both conciliatory sheep and façades will be consolidated by these systems. They give a complete duplicate of an authentic framework that is prepared for assailants, like the conciliatory sheep framework, and at the same time (like façades) they are fluently available and hard to sidestep. The honeypot innovation is additionally utilized for concentrating on spam and email reaping exercises. Honeypots have been conveyed to concentrate on how spammers distinguish open mail transfers. To find out the reasons why spam messages were received, spam emails are received and broken down. Likewise, by utilizing an email address, an email trap can be set up, committed simply to getting spam messages.

1.3.2 Strategies of honeypot deployment

The organization ought to deliberately want to amplify the qualities of honeypots and minimize the dangers involved. At that point, assault-related data can be gathered by the honeypot. Nonetheless, if an effective attack happens on the honeypot inside the system, that compromised honeypot system may be exploited to check for other potential flaws in the system. This is the primary issue of initiating the honeypot inside the creation framework. This would not happen in other honeypot arrangement techniques as the entire honeynet can itself be an invented system (Abduvaliyev, Pathan, Zhou, Roman and Wong 2013). A specific measure of information, for example the site core of a web server, may have to be reproduced in the honeypot to cover the honeypot. Another strategy is to assemble a honeynet, which is a system of honeypots that mimics and imitates an authentic system.

1.4 JUSTIFICATION

The current work introduces the honeypot framework aided by the IDS. These techniques are regarded as the main terms for defensive functions. This methodology is also regarded as the flexible security mechanism, and it also eliminates the stealing of information by attackers. The proposed methodology includes the main functionalities in order to confuse attackers as well as gather the framework's information, then direct them onto the wrong path. This process differentiates the attacker's movements with new techniques and applications. The intruders may have a place within the black hat group and attempt to take over the information that was stolen from the framework, aided by data like the TCP address, IP address, and so on. After gaining information about the attacker, the next action of the honeypot framework will be to protect the user's information and secure the information from the attackers. The honeypot framework plays a major role in identifying intruders.

1.5 OUTLINE OF THE CHAPTERS

Chapter 1 describes the introduction of the topic, the background, problems identified, etc.

Chapter 2 gives a review of recent literature on the topic.

Chapter 3 depicts the inspiration for this examination/target work.

Chapter 4 delineates a major technique for honeypots utilizing intrusion detection systems.

Chapter 5 depicts an ant-based DDoS detection technique using roaming virtual honeypots.

Chapter 6 discloses how to upgrade intrusion detection system performance by using a FireCol Protection Services-based honeypot system.

Chapter 7 delineates the Efficient Approach to Protect the Network and Intrusion Prevention (EIDPS).

Chapter 8 clarifies an effective ODAIDS-HPS approach for preventing, detecting and responding to DDoS attacks.

Chapter 9 is the conclusion of this work and recommends some conceivable future improvements.

CHAPTER 2

LITERATURE SURVEY

2.1 INTRODUCTION

Intrusion detection is a major part of wired and wireless sensor networks. Intrusions will occur due to the dangers in and attacks on the networks. To prevent these intrusions, many intrusion detection techniques such as present or system located, initial or irregularity located, energetic or submissive observing, concurrent or interlude processing and, finally, integrated or circulated applications have been presented. IDS has become a necessity due to the significance of preserving privacy and obtaining reliability for our most appreciated possession, which is data. Many research papers have been published based on these intrusion detection techniques.

In this chapter, related research works on IDSs are presented. Here, these related works are classified as follows:

1) Anomaly-based IDS
2) Distributed approach for IDS
3) Trust-based IDS
4) Cluster-based IDS
5) Intelligent IDS
6) IDS in MANET
7) IDS for Heterogeneous WSNs
8) Game theoretic approaches for ID
9) IDS for various attacks
10) Agent-based IDS
11) Traffic analysis-based IDS
12) Immunity-based IDS
13) Optimized algorithms used for IDS
14) Data mining approaches for IDS
15) Energy-efficient IDS

2.2 ANOMALY-BASED IDS

Intrusion detection is concerned with detecting executions that make an effort to violate information security. The security policy of an information system is violated by the intrusion, which is an activity. IDS, therefore, is an attempt aimed at curtailing the excesses of the intruders. IDS is either misuse-based or anomaly-based depending on the model of its application. Idowu *et al.* (2013) have projected a new but vigorous algorithm called a membrane algorithm for NP-complete optimization problem solving using the P-system paradigm. Systems try to prevent intrusion attempts, and the IDS is neither needed nor anticipated by the monitoring system. Logging details about incidents and recording trials is the main ID and prevention system for attainable incident identification. For other desires, like issues' identification with security strategies and discouraging singles and previously documented threats from overstepping security strategies, Intrusion Detection and Prevention Systems (IDPSs) are additionally used by organizations. Given the security infrastructure of every organization, IDPSs have become essential. Jabez and Muthukumar (2015) have proposed an innovative scheme named "outlier detection", where the irregularity of the dataset is estimated by the NOF.

El-Alfy and Al-Obeidat (2014) have proposed a scheme for "anomaly-based intrusion detection" using a "fuzzy classification" scheme together with a selection of greedy parameters. Based on the content, time and host, the projected method attributes have superiority in dealing with different kinds of attributes and compressing TCP/IP network traffic basic packet headers. At the same time, the selection of the greedy parameter algorithm allows the selection of the finest attribute group that was most significantly aimed at detecting intrusive events to decrease the dimensional and computational complexity, and different network components of the constructed system are enabled to be virtual in order to develop open system infrastructures such as radar links, informal wireless links, and cloud calculating and shrewd networks.

Modeling normal user activities is an important issue in intrusion irregularity detection. The technique of conventional data mining is applied generally to finite audit datasets for the purpose of normal behavior extraction from user activities. In audit datasets, these methods model stagnant user behavior. Park *et al.* (2010) have projected an "anomaly intrusion detection" scheme which uninterruptedly uses the normal behavior of an operator above the review file stream. A set of characters is used to represent the features of a movement in this paper. Each cluster, in the proposed method, represents the regularity scale of the actions with respect to the feature. To improve the performance of irregularity detection, different statistics of actions corresponding to the detected clusters were also demonstrated in this paper.

When detecting a new attack, irregularity intrusion detection plays a significant part in an IDS by identifying any variation from the normal profile. Lin *et al.* (2012) have projected an efficient algorithm with a selection of features and decision rules applied to irregularity or "asymmetry intrusion detection". The benefits of "simulated annealing" (SA), the "decision tree" (DT), and SVM are taken as key ideas in this paper. SA and SVM can find the best-chosen attributes to increase the accuracy of irregularity intrusion detection in the proposed algorithm. The decision rules for new attacks are obtained by analyzing the information after expending SA, the KDD'99 dataset and the DT, and the accuracy of classification also improved in this paper. In addition, SA spontaneously adjusted the best restriction settings for the DT and SVM.

El-Ghali and Masri (2009) have presented a new method for identifying failures of software security, the major aim of which is simplifying the detection and restoration of security weaknesses. The proposed method of this paper depended on the online capture of performances and profiling, offline performance replay and evaluation. The flow analysis, known as a "fine-grained dynamic data flow analysis", was engaged by this proposed approach in combination with anomaly detection. The proposed goal of this paper, also called "information flow anomaly detection", was detected in various security failures, including ones that concern intrusions of privacy and ones that do not. A prototype tool called DynFlow implemented the method for Java byte code programs.

The security of the WSN is an important objective for many researchers. IDSs played a major role in detecting and avoiding security attacks. Maleh *et al.* (2015) have presented a hybrid, inconsequential intrusion detection system. To reduce energy consumption, their IDS worked on the superiority of cluster-based architecture. This system used anomaly detection and a group of signature rules to identify mischievous behaviors and afford a global lightweight IDS based on the "SVM algorithm".

Sun *et al.* (2013) have presented a combination of ID and "system monitoring modules" in the background of WSNs. To identify corrupted data, they proposed an extended Kalman filter (EKF)-based appliance. Specifically, by monitoring the activities of its neighbors and by using the

EKF to forecast their future situations (real in-network aggregated standards), each node aimed to fix a normal range of upcoming transmitted collected values. Due to the potential coarse environs, high packet loss rate and recognized insecurity, this task is challenging. The authors explained how to utilize the EKF to solve the challenge of making valuable local detection mechanisms. They presented how to obtain an abstract inception by means of diverse combination utilities (mean, total, maximum, and minimum). They also applied an algorithm integrating progressive summation and a generalized possibility ratio to improve detection understanding. Finally, they explained how they offered native discovery methods that work mutually with the "system monitoring module" to distinguish between mischievous actions and reserve actions to overwhelm the restrictions of native discovery mechanisms.

The difficulties of misinterpretation, misdetection and the absence of a real-time reaction to the outbreak are the most significant challenges to intrusion detection. For intrusion detection, numerous information excavating methods are used, such as grouping, cataloging and union law recognition. The anticipated hybrid method of the paper offered by Ravale *et al.* (2015) combined information excavating methods such as the RBF kernel function and the K-means clustering algorithm of the Support Vector Machine as a sorting unit. Reducing the number of features related to each data point was the central point of the projected method in this paper. In terms of detection rate and accuracy, the suggested method worked well when employed with the KDDCUP'99 dataset.

In WSNs, safety matters are most important. WSNs are vulnerable to certain kinds of occurrences as they are composed of inexpensive and minor devices and are positioned in exposed and isolated surroundings. Yan *et al.* (2010) have suggested an IDS formed in the sphere of the group head. The suggested IDS was a hybrid IDS. It had variances as well as an abuse finding unit. The aim of this paper was to increase the finding rate and reduce the untrue progressive degree by utilizing the benefits of abuse finding and variance finding. However, an executive element was used to assimilate the identified outcomes and to state the kinds of occurrences.

2.3 DISTRIBUTED APPROACH FOR IDS

Krishnan (2015) has conveyed that a dispersed self-adjusting IDS depends on designable mobile factors that can represent a vital link in the defense against major security assaults. Krishnan has presented an "intrusion detection model" that is prepared as a blend of the two forms of IDS: the rule-based and the behavior-based schemes. The advantages of both the host-based and network-based IDSs were drawn out by this model, which deploys them prudently and considers the serious features of MANETs. This was an effective framework, conscious of the integral restrictions of MANETs, and is self-adjusting in its nature, unlike many projected and implemented IDSs. Furthermore, the practice of lightweight mobile agents provided a little overhead mechanism that was extremely suitable for MANETs' characteristics.

Gaussian-distributed WSNs can provide differentiated detection skills in different places, but the related work is limited. Wang, Fu and Agrawal (2013) examined the issue of ID in a "Gaussian-distributed WSN" by describing the detection possibility regarding the application requirements and the system factors in terms of both single-sensing detection and multiple-sensing recognition scenarios. The effects of several system parameters upon the probability of detection are also observed in this paper.

The probability of detection is the same for any point in a WSN with a constant distribution. Differentiated detection capabilities at different locations can be provided by Gaussian-distributed WSNs. Gaussian-distributed WSNs are highly organized in practice. Wang *et al.* (2013) examined the issue of ID in a Gaussian-distributed WSN by describing the probability of ID in respect of network arrangement factors and intrusion distance. This paper considered two detection models: single-sensing detection and multiple-sensing detection. The projected method examined the effects of several system factors on the intrusion detection probability. This work allowed them to systematically formulate the probability of ID within a defined intrusion distance within different application scenarios.

Nowadays, wireless technology has become very important because of its possible usage in remote sites for public, educational, scientific, and military purposes and security, including intrusion detection and invasion avoidance. Distributed wireless sensor networks have problems with detecting and avoiding malevolent nodes, which constantly get destructive threats and compromise numerous sensor nodules. Therefore, for sensor identity and message transmission purposes, sensor networks need to sustain an authentication facility. Intrusion detection and intrusion prevention systems, which are always used in sensor security applications, can improve system safety by discovering destructive or compromised nodules. Fathinavid (2012) has projected an energy-aware procedure for intrusion detection in WSNs. The detection system applied in this paper was based on an autonomous learning concept.

When evaluating the intrusion detection ability of a WSN, the node arrangement method plays a pivotal role. Even a random arrangement approach fails to afford further security to delicate zones in the linkage. However, further precautions for the main zones in the system range were provided by a Gaussian deployment strategy. Additionally, all the distribution policies suffer from problems of energy waste. Ghosal and Halder (2013) developed a tailor-made Gaussian deployment strategy reducing issues of energy waste. This paper inspected the intrusion detection issue in adapted Gaussian distributed networks, such as the use of both multiple-sensing and single-sensing recognition circumstances below a genuine probabilistic detecting pattern. A broad simulation was completed to authenticate the accuracy of the modeling and analysis. The effects of the various system factors on the recognition possibility are also detected. By associating its equivalent Gaussian deployment approach under the considered circumstances, the usefulness of the proposed method was established.

Medhat *et al.* (2017) have presented an effective intrusion detection model. Intelligent techniques were used to detect intrusions in this model. This paper introduced two designs. The levels of the sensor node, sink node, and base station were represented by the first design. The levels of the sensor node and sink nodes were represented by the second design. This paper also proposed two intrusion detection algorithms: one used a managed learning mechanism to be used on the level of the sensor node, and the other used an unconfirmed learning mechanism to be used on the levels of the base station and the sink node. The output of the algorithms was a set of recognition rules that are structured in the form of dual tree. High recognition correctness using a smaller number of selected structures was provided by the introduced algorithms.

Security issues are of major importance due to the dangerous nature of such applications. Since WSNs are often organized in aggressive and vulnerable environments, they are susceptible to various kinds of occurrences. Livani and Abadi (2010) have offered a new scattered intrusion detection method, known as PCADID, for discovering routing attacks in WSNs. They subdivided a WSN into clusters of sensor nodes in the projected method in this paper. Certain nodes were designated as observer nodes that collaborate with one another to constitute a universal standard outline in each group. Using a principal component analysis (PCA), all observer nodes established a sub-profile for private normal network traffic. Based on all received sub-profiles, each observer node composed a universal standard outline. Every monitor node used the profile to identify irregularities in the private network traffic. The normal global profile was reorganized according to the normal network's performance alterations over time. This paper established that PCADID accomplished a high detection accuracy level with a low false alarm rate, however it reduces the memory and power consumption in the system.

To detect malicious attackers, many critical WSNs require an effective, lightweight and flexible "intrusion detection system". Li *et al.* (2008) have projected an IDS based on a dispersed cluster that meets all the above needs by segregating the sensor networks into numerous clusters. The sensors were actually close to each other and were prepared with similar sensing capability. To detect malicious attackers, the intrusion detection algorithm in this paper took multiple features of the sensor nodes into consideration simultaneously. The projected system in this paper decreased the "false alarm rate" and improved the "detection accuracy rate" (Li *et al.* 2008).

Li *et al.* (2012) supposed that the scenario includes multiple facilities. A Reverse Gaussian distribution resulted from the two-dimensional Gaussian distribution, and sensors were organized following a Reverse Gaussian distribution. The detection probability was improved by employing a greater amount of sensor nodes on the boundary. As intrusion attacks begin from the boundary zone, the Reverse Gaussian deployment method provided a good security performance with the same amount of investment compared to existing deployment methods.

2.4 TRUST-BASED IDS

Within WSNs, the detection of inconsistencies is critical for the smooth functioning of the network. An intrusion detection system based on the calculation of trust of the adjoining nodule was projected by Sajjad *et al.* (2015), who proposed an IDS in which every node observes the trust point of its adjoining nodules. Neighboring nodes might be acknowledged as risky, trustworthy, or malicious based on those trust values. For packet forwarding purposes, reliable nodes were suggested to the progressing engine. Selective forwarding attacks, jamming attacks and hello flood attacks were identified by examining the system measurements and malicious node behavior in the projected system.

Prevention, detection and mitigation are the three main components that deal with the security of a wireless sensor network. But it is very hard to protect a wireless sensor network from malicious attacks all the time. Dhakne and Chatur (2015) have planned a DTBID method that considers several elements for creating trust in a sensor node. Trust, which is distributed among other features such as energy, reliability, data, etc., was measured in this paper for intrusion detection. The authors derived and formulated forms of trust such as direct trust, approval trust, and incidental trust from these factors. Also, they provide a method in this paper to decide whether a particular node is malicious or not by associating the particular trust derived from their intrusion detection technique to that of objective trust, which is calculated based on the real data of every node without deliberating on the system forces at work, such node mobility, trust decay over time, and any malicious attacks. This paper considered a sensor node as malicious when there is a lot of difference between the individual trust derived from their model compared to the objective trust.

Bao *et al.* (2012) have projected a hierarchical trust management procedure based on a highly-scalable cluster for WSNs to deal with selfish or malicious nodes efficiently. This paper considered multidimensional trust qualities resulting from communication and social networks to calculate the overall trust of a sensor node. The authors also defined a varied WSN containing a huge amount of sensor nodes with a large number of social and QoS performances with the aim of producing a "ground truth" node position with the help of a novel probability model. This helped as a foundation for authenticating their procedure strategy by associating the subjective trust obtained because of the protocol's implementation at runtime against the objective trust gained from the actual node position. This paper applied this to trust-based geographic routing and a trust management protocol-based ID to demonstrate its utility. This paper identified the best trust arrangement and composition for each application to maximize application performance. The authors discovered that there exists an optimal trust threshold for reducing false positives and false negatives for intrusion detection based on trust.

Bao *et al.* (2011) have projected an IDS based on trust using a highly-scalable hierarchical trust management procedure for clustered wireless sensor networks. This paper included a trust metric considering both QoS trust and social trust to detect malicious nodes. Each cluster head applied intrusion detection based on trust to measure the trustworthiness and maliciousness of sensor nodes in its cluster by statistically investigating the peer-to-peer trust estimation results collected from sensor nodes. The base station estimated the cluster heads. Aimed at a critical estimation of the projected trust-based IDS, this paper developed a systematic model based on stochastic Petri nets, along with a statistical process for computing the false alarm probability. This paper investigated the understanding of false alarms with regard to the lowest trust threshold according to which a node was considered malicious. The results of this paper showed that there exists a best trust threshold for decreasing false positives and false negatives.

Gheorghe *et al.* (2012) have projected the Adaptive Trust Management Protocol, which corrects trust and reputation depending on node behavior. The protocol includes three phases: the Learning phase, the Exchanging phase and the Updating phase. Experience of the Learning phase is calculated based on warnings received from TinyAFD. Experience associations between neighboring nodes were replaced in the Exchanging phase. Based on experience, trust and reputation were simplified in the Updating phase. To estimate the evolution of experience, trust and reputation, the ATMP was executed on top of TinyOS and was verified via TOSSIM in numerous attack situations. Due to its incorporation with a complex IDS, this work covered a larger range of attacks.

2.5 CLUSTER-BASED IDS

To classify malicious attackers, several mission critical WSNs need an effective, flexible and lightweight intrusion detection system. Li *et al.* (2008) projected an intrusion detection system based on a distributed group. By partitioning the sensor systems attached to various clusters, the scheme met all the above requirements wherein the sensors in every cluster are actually near to each other and are equipped with a similar detecting capability. In order to detect malicious attackers precisely, the proposed intrusion detection system takes numerous attributes of the sensor nodes into consideration concurrently. The projected algorithm in this paper decreased the false alarm level and increased the detection accuracy compared to current intrusion detection methods while reducing the computation and transmission power consumption.

Wang *et al.* (2011) have suggested a method of IDS formed in a CWSN. The proposed IDS was an IIDS. This requires the system to avoid intrusions and work instantaneously by examining the occurrences. The three individual IDSs that were incorporated in the IIDS were IDS, Hybrid IDS (HIDS) and Intelligent HIDS (IHIDS). These corresponded to the various proficiencies and prospects of occurrences anticipated for the sink nodes, cluster-head nodes and sensor nodes. The proposed IIDS in this paper entailed an anomaly and a misuse detection module. The objective of this paper was to increase the detection rate and lessen the false rates of misuse detection and anomaly detection.

For safety-sensitive WSNs, authenticating the validity and reliability of the distributed information is essential. Su *et al.* (2007) have planned a hybrid security scheme, named the eHIP system, which combines intrusion prevention with intrusion detection to provide an energy-efficient and protected cluster-based WSN. The eHIP system contains a collaboration-based intrusion detection (CID) sub-system and an authentication-based intrusion prevention (AIP) sub-system. To improve energy efficiency, both sub-systems provided varied appliances for several security demands in CWSN. In order to authenticate control messages and detected files, two different verification mechanisms were introduced in the AIP to avoid external attacks. These dual verification mechanisms were accordingly modified to be consistent with the comparative position of the data enclosed in the control messages and detected files. CID was proposed in this paper since the security risk from compromised sensor nodes cannot be entirely avoided by AIP. To balance the trade-off between network security and energy efficiency, the idea of collaborative monitoring was recommended in CID. Academic investigations and recreations of AIP and CID were also offered in this book so as to assess the presentation of the eHIP system.

In serious circumstances like military and commercial efforts, there is enormous potential for WSNs to be employed. Yet these applications, in which the nodes and communication networks are targets for aggressors, are frequently essential when deployed in aggressive environments. This makes WSNs susceptible to a range of possible occurrences. Predictable safety mechanisms are not valid because of their features. Sedjelmaci *et al.* (2012) have recommended an IDS for a CWSN that aims to unite the benefits of anomaly and signal recognition, which are high detection levels and low false positives, respectively.

2.6 INTELLIGENT IDS

The security and privacy of information are two of the major concerns for today's embedded devices. The basic safety methods of the signature-based discovery of malware and even updates of a signature database are not possible resolutions as they cannot protect such systems, as they effectively have restricted resources. The system must be capable of discovering and preventing any type of intrusion before the network is weakened by the attackers, with the aim of operating wireless embedded devices in a protected mode. Saeed *et al.* (2016) have offered an ID scheme by applying an intelligent safety construction using RNN. It was executed for an existing WSN system, and its component was virtually established by effectively identifying the existence of any suspicious sensor node and irregular activity in the base station with great precision and minimal performance overheads to authenticate the potentiality of the proposed security system.

In their paper, Tian and Gao (2009) offer an intelligent community intrusion detection system based on a WSN and a fuzzy neural network. This system was composed of Advanced RISC Machines (ARMs), data acquisition nodes, wireless mesh networks and a control center. Sensors were used in the data acquisition node to gather data. Then the data acquisition node administered them with an image detection algorithm, before data are diffused to the control center by the wireless mesh network. The system starts the camera, and the FNN is used to recognize the face's image when there is an unusual occurrence. This paper created the configuration of the FNN, and, to instruct the FNN, they embraced the Levenberg-Marquart enhancing algorithm, thus improving the convergence rate and the recognition accuracy. The recognition methods can accurately categorize the face by using the skill of strong self-learning and the non-linear function method of the fuzzy neural network.

While emerging technology has transformed the environment of surveillance and monitoring applications, the sensory data collected by these devices still remain changeable and weakly harmonized. Pramod *et al.* (2009) have described a study task called "In2DS" for remote surveillance and monitoring applications that can significantly advance the present systems in terms of energy, cost and performance. The impulse for developing In2DS comes from the fact that WSNs can offer extensive sensing analysis, night and severe climate observation, multi-sensor data fusion and in-network data administering, thereby improving current intrusion detection abilities and refining alarm functionalities. Pramod *et al.* (2009) offered some initial results based on field experimentations carried out as part of the project and provided a thorough examination of Passive Infra-Red (PIR) sensor detection performance.

2.7 IDS IN MANET

IDSs for MANETs need constant checking, which leads to the quick reduction of a node's battery life. Subba *et al.* (2016) have projected a novel IDS system containing a new cluster leader selection procedure and a hybrid IDS to address this problem. The Vickrey-Clarke-Groves device was used to select the cluster leader that provides the intrusion detection service. A threshold-based lightweight module and a powerful anomaly-based heavyweight module made up the hybrid IDS. Initially, only the lightweight module was triggered. The decision to trigger the heavyweight module was taken by modeling the ID method as an incomplete information non-cooperative game between the selected leader node and the possible malicious node. The IDS traffic and overall power consumption were reduced by these algorithms, which also maintained a high and precise detection rate.

Even though mobile devices are turning out to be the most common tool for connection, practices supporting mobility are a serious source of concern, for the reason that their initial design did not provide strong security. Andreolini *et al.* (2014) have presented a new class of stealth network attacks, known as mobility-based evasion, where an attacker breaches a malicious payload in such a manner that no part can be acknowledged by existing defensive mechanisms, including the most modern network IDSs working in a safe mode. They offered an original cooperative structure for intrusion detection that can prevent mobility-based evasion.

2.8 IDSs FOR HETEROGENEOUS WSNs

In many applications, such as identifying an invader on a battlefield, intrusion detection in WSNs can be useful. The ID is used to detect the existence of inappropriate, incorrect, or abnormal moving invaders for a WSN. It is therefore important to describe the WSN's limitations, for instance, node density and sensing range in terms of a desirable detection probability. Wang *et al.* (2008) measured these problems corresponding to two WSN models: homogenous and heterogeneous WSNs. They also derived the detection probability by bearing in mind two sensing models: single-sensing detection and multiple-sensing detection. Network connectivity and transmission reachability are also essential aspects to safeguard the corresponding detection probability in a WSN. These are also deliberated upon in this paper.

To execute various surveillance tasks, for example, search, rescue, target tracking, and a variety of tasks in smart situations, WSNs are increasingly being used in diverse surroundings. Node localization is naturally one of the system parameters in such tasks. Node localization is needed to report on the cause of events, support group querying of sensors, routing and to reply to requests on the network coverage. Ahmed and Rajeswari (2012) have appraised different methods of node localization detection in wireless sensor networks.

Heterogeneous networks are rising fast at the moment, and are being established and arranged by governments as well as private companies.

Heterogeneous networks are affected because of the distance, mobility, and behavior of nodes. Many methods have been tried in order to overcome this. For example, Rajkumar and Vayanaperumal (2015) have projected a Leader Based IDS. This technique aims to recognize and prevent DOS along with other incidences, such as Sybil and sinkhole attacks, in networks by deploying the Leader Based IDS into access points in the networks. This approach applies three basic safety tasks: authentication, positive incentive provision and the prevention of DOS. Packet verification and IP verification were also considered in this paper for the improvement of the efficiency of the diverse networks.

2.9 GAME THEORETIC APPROACHES FOR ID

Shen *et al.* (2011) adopted the distributed-centralized network wherein every sensor node equips an IDS agent, but only the IDS agent that exists in the cluster head (CH) with adequate energy will launch. In order to build an intrusion detection game demonstrating the interactions between a malicious sensor node and a CH-IDS agent, the signaling game was applied and its balances for the optimal detection approach were also required. The paper illustrated the stage intrusion detection game at precise periods in aspects of its performer's efficacies, pure-strategy Bayesian-Nash equilibrium (BNE) and mixed-strategy BNE. The CH-IDS agent did not permanently employ the defense strategy under these BNEs and, as a result, the power of CH can be protected. The stage intrusion detection game developed into a multi-stage dynamic intrusion detection game wherein, based on Bayesian rules, the beliefs on the malicious sensor node could be updated as the game evolved. The best response strategy for the CH-IDS agent could be obtained from the current belief and the perfect Bayesian equilibrium (PBE). Subsequently, an intrusion detection mechanism and a corresponding algorithm were projected.

Patel *et al.* (2013) have offered a game theoretic method, namely Game-based Fuzzy Q-Learning (G-FQL). A combination of both the game theory method and FQL is permitted by G-FQL in WSNs. G-FQL is a three-player strategy game consisting of sink nodes, a base station, and an attacker. In WSNs, the game performs any time a victim node in the network accepts a flooding packet as a DDoS attack beyond a specific alarm event threshold. The projected model of this paper implements cooperative defense counter-attack scenarios for the base station and sink node to work as rational decision-maker players through a game theory approach.

In order to portray the game parameters and exhibit the player's intentions, the security requirements of WSNs are taken into account. The game data is not supposed to be wholly known to the players, who take a robust optimization approach to address this vagueness of the data to simplify the problem. Illustrative examples of the established game model were put forward in the paper by Moosavi and Bui (2014) for measuring the authority and efficiency of the framework. An equilibrium analysis exposed how the inconsistent aims of the intruder and IDS force them to assume different conventional attitudes toward data insecurity.

Estiri and Khademzadeh (2010) have projected a game theory-based technique to strengthen an IDS in WSNs. This paper also concentrated on reducing packet attacks that are a weak point in WSNs. First, they restricted the malicious nodes and then gave them incentives to mend their ways and try to perform in support of other nodes in the WSN, so the authors of this paper claim that their model is also a correctional model. It proposed the attack-defense problem as a non-cooperative, two-player, non-zero-sum game between an attacker and a WSN. Based on such a supposition that sensor nodes are rational, this paper projected a repeated game model of dropping packets, which are attack-proof beside DPAs. By starting a subgame perfect periodic collusion-resistant punishment appliance, the model prevented malicious nodes from attacking. To reach a cooperative Nash equilibrium, the model encouraged sensor networks. This paper showed that the model was partially collusion resistant, once the malicious nodes inhabited less than the majority of the network.

Estiri and Khademzadeh (2010) have proposed a technique for an IDS in WSNs. This paper concentrated on dropping packet attacks (DPAs) in WSNs and also concentrated on the project of security enforcement mechanisms for avoiding attacks. This paper offered a dynamic game-theoretic model to investigate "intrusion detection" in WSNs. A signaling model was used in this paper to model the connections between points of a wireless sensor network. The authors observed the interaction between an aggressor and an individual node as a Bayesian game with partial data, and created models for such a game. By reaching Nash equilibrium, this paper proved the legitimacy of the projected model.

2.10 IDS FOR VARIOUS ATTACKS

Inadequate hardware resources, for instance memory size and battery life, congenitally limit wireless sensor nodes. In terms of the addition of security mechanisms to protect sensor nodes, these aspects impact the lifespan of wireless sensor networks and pose numerous issues. Defending sensor nodes from malicious occurrences has become increasingly more important as the number of requests using wireless sensor networks rises. Huang *et al.* (2013) have projected a novel intrusion detection system known as the Markovian IDS to guard sensor nodes against malicious occurrences. To define the best security approaches, the Markovian IDS merged game theory with anomaly and misuse detection. To forecast future attack patterns and implement suitable measures, the Markovian IDS also employed Markov decision procedures with an attack-pattern-mining algorithm.

For numerous task-critical applications, WSNs' security is becoming a major concern. The work in the paper by Sarigiannidis *et al.* (2015) focused on how to protect against a particularly dangerous form of attack, the Sybil attack. By disrupting many networking protocols, Sybil attacks can severely depreciate the system's performance and compromise its security. Sarigiannidis *et al.* have offered a rule-based anomaly detection system, known as RADS, that monitors and detects Sybil attacks in significant WSNs. In order to accomplish the anomaly detection tasks, the projected system of this paper relied on an ultra-wideband (UWB) ranging-based detection algorithm that functioned in a distributed manner, needing no cooperation or data sharing between the sensor nodes. The probability of the proposed method was confirmed analytically, while the performance of RADS in revealing Sybil attacks was extensively evaluated both mathematically and numerically.

Guerroumi *et al.* (2015) have offered an IDS against sinkhole attacks in WSNs with mobile sinks. The network area was divided into a flat grid of cells in the detection model, and this paper used the signature-based technique, which was denoted by the detection rate of a cell, to distinguish between real and false sink nodes. The projected IDS considered two types of sink mobility: periodic and random. The additional energy consumption incurred by the IDS was low as the cell leaders did not stimulate their IDS agent concurrently.

2.11 AGENT-BASED IDS

The aim of "intrusion detection" is to differentiate between misuse and anomaly performance in an attempt to safeguard protected, dependable network processes and facilities. ID is best conveyed by "multi-agent system" tools and progressive workout systems. Currently, to generate IDPSs, different soft computing and machine learning techniques in terms of computational intelligence have been developed. Shamshirband *et al.*

(2013) have put forward an analysis and classification of existing IDPS patterns in charge of traditional artificial computational intelligence with multi-agent support. In this analysis, the importance of the procedures and policies and their presentation and restrictions are also examined. The boundaries are treated as challenges in order to get a collection of requirements for IDPSs in launching a Co-WIDPS architectural project.

Over the past few years, WSNs have turned into one of the most encouraging and interesting research areas. But WSNs are susceptible, due to their constrained resources, to various kinds of attacks such as DoS attacks, which result in a huge number of compromised nodes. It is important to preserve basic security for the successful operation of universal WSNs. However, there is no active intrusion detection and self-recovery system to remove the harm of DoS attacks. An "agent-based ID" and self-recovery system for WSNs was projected in a paper by Sun and Liu (2013) to solve this problem. The projected method adopted distributed architecture to observe intrusion activities and recognize abnormal event processing in local nodes. The simulation results of this paper specified that the compromised nodes could self-recover effectively, and the network's entire energy consumption is also concentrated efficiently.

2.12 TRAFFIC ANALYSIS-BASED IDS

Zhijie and Ruchuang (2012) have projected an efficient traffic prediction algorithm for sensor nodes that utilizes the Markov model. To discover the attacks which have more of an influence on packet traffic, such as selective forwarding attacks and DOS attacks, a distributed anomaly detection scheme, TPID (Traffic Prediction-based Intrusion Detection), was designed based on a traffic prediction algorithm. In TPID, each node acts autonomously when predicting traffic and discovering an anomaly.

Ponomarchuk and Seo (2010) have projected a lightweight, fast, and effective "traffic intensity-based intrusion detection method" for WSNs, comprising a large number of nodules which transfer data periodically. The intrusion detection technique was centered on the investigation of the neighbor's actions and the thresholding method, and was applied to particular parameters: the number of received packets in a timeframe of a given length and the inter-arrival time of packets. The installation of supplementary hardware and further communication costs are not required by this method. The proposed technique of this paper used both hierarchical and flat WSNs. For each traffic parameter, this paper contained proposals for the choice of the threshold value. The outcomes of this paper, which was performed in a Castalia emulator for WSNs, established that the projected intrusion detection technique was more accurate in comparison with common algorithms.

2.13 IMMUNITY-BASED IDS

It is enormously challenging to categorize malicious behavior by means of conventional intrusion detection systems in WSNs due to the distributed nature of DoS attacks. To confront this, Shamshirband *et al.* (2014) have proposed a bio-inspired technique, named the Cooperative-based Fuzzy Artificial Immune System (Co-FAIS). The danger theory of the human immune system inspired its modular-based defense approach. To compute the irregularity of sensor behavior in terms of context antigen value (CAV) or attackers, the agents coordinated and worked with one another and updated the fuzzy activation threshold for its security reaction. The sniffer module was modified to the sink node to review information by examining the packet components and sending the log file to the next level in such a multi-node scenario. The Fuzzy Misuse Detector Module (FMDM) incorporated a danger detector unit to recognize the sources of danger signals. The infected sources are transferred to the Fuzzy Q-learning Vaccination Modules (FQVMs), in order for specific, essential actions to take place to improve system capabilities. To create optimum defense strategies, the Cooperative Decision Making Modules (Co-DMMs) combined the danger detector module with the FQVMs. The Low Energy Adaptive Clustering Hierarchy (LEACH) was simulated by a system emulator in this paper to estimate the performance of the projected model.

Since WSNs are distributed in unattended surroundings and have limited energy, storage and computational abilities, they are susceptible to various attacks. Protective techniques can be applied to guard WSNs against certain types of attacks. However, in the case of certain attacks, preventative methods are not effective. Hence it is essential to develop particular mechanisms for intrusion detection. Due to the traditional intrusion detection algorithm's resource limitations, it cannot be applied directly to WSNs. Liu and Yu (2008) projected a new IDS, based on immunology, which is distributed, robust, and adaptive, consistent with the problems in the existing intrusion detection systems.

Zhao and Liu (2011) have designed a dynamic "immunity-based intrusion detection model" for WSNs to improve their security. The generation of detector and antigen detection was accomplished by the projected model of this paper. The self-model class was introduced to filter the self-element and reduce the workload of the detector in the process of antigen detection. The prototype realized the dynamic evolution of self-sets, the dynamic evolution of non-mature detectors, mature detectors and memory detectors in the process of detector generation. At the same time, in order to advance the range of antibodies, vaccine extraction and vaccination technology were applied.

2.14 OPTIMIZED ALGORITHMS USED FOR IDS

The identification and protection of attacks is a hard problem to tackle in the network security field (Sandhya & Julian 2014). To ensure network security, an operative IDS is necessary. To discover useful patterns of system features, IDSs contain pattern analysis techniques. Anomalies were calculated by means of the group of relevant system features. The derived patterns comprise inputs of classification systems. Clustering methods are useful for the recognition of unknown attack patterns. The identification of substantially reduced input features was offered by genetic algorithm-based clustering. Sandhya and Julian have thus presented a theoretical outline for detecting attacks for intrusion detection by applying the genetic "K-means algorithm".

In order to thwart an attacker from introducing compromised nodules so as to destroy or else interrupt network performance, it is necessary for WSNs to have security methods in place. Rong *et al.* (2011) have offered an ID process for wireless detector systems that does not need prior knowledge of network behavior or a learning phase to establish this knowledge. A more practical method was proposed in the paper by Rong *et al.* (2011). This procedure was created with small to medium-size networks in mind, such as home or office networks. The proposed algorithm was also dynamic in nature so as to manage unknown and new attack types. This algorithm aimed to protect the network and safeguard consistent and accurate sensor analyses.

Sajana *et al.* (2009) have offered a low-complexity process for intrusion detection in the presence of clutter arising from wind-blown vegetation, using "Passive Infra-Red" (PIR) sensors in a WSN. The algorithm of this paper was based on a combination of Support-Vector-Machine (SVM) and Haar Transform (HT)-based training and was field-tested in a network system containing about 15-20 sensing nodes. This paper also contained a closed-form expression for the signal produced by an attacker moving at a constant velocity. The algorithm shows how this expression can be exploited to control the course of motion information and the velocity of the intruder from the signals of three well-placed sensors.

2.15 DATA MINING APPROACH FOR IDS

In respect of preventing attacks against secure computer networks, IDSs can be seen as a secondary source of protection, and they accompany the security basics that are implemented. Stringent requirements for the design of IDSs are necessitated by the unusual characteristics of a WSN. Coppolino *et al.* (2013) have planned a hybrid, lightweight, distributed IDS for WSNs. This IDS uses both misuse-based and anomaly-based detection methods. It is comprised of a number of Local Agents running lighter anomaly-based detection methods on the motes and a Central Agent, which performs extremely accurate ID by using data mining techniques. In the detection method of the Central Agent, decision trees have been approved as the cataloging algorithm. The decision trees' behavior has also been examined in particular attack scenarios.

Data Aggregation (DA) is a method of data gathering in WSNs. It delivers benefits such as recording consolidated data, reducing data redundancy, improving the network lifespan, etc. Vamsi and Kant (2015) have projected a new secure DA method. By means of TMS at the node level and IDS at the BS (Base Station) side, this paper presents a secure data aggregation framework for WSNs. Each nodule in the network executes network activities, for instance, cluster head selection, data aggregation, and reporting to the BS, and each nodule also measures the performance of its neighbors using trust ratings. The BS examines the received data using IDS and reports the data concerning the malicious activity back to nodules in the system. After the data aggregation process, the suggested model recognizes and separates the malicious nodes.

Zhang *et al.* (2009) have given a scalable dynamic key management scheme for WSNs wherein new nodes can join a sensor network securely, and then compromised nodules can be isolated from the system in time. The framework of this paper does not rely on such infrastructure as base stations and robots, unlike centralized and location-based key management schemes. This paper unites proficiently with the "cluster-based IDS" and upgrades the total security of a WSN.

WSNs are developing as cost-effective resolutions for crucial applications such as the remote monitoring of strategic installations covering pollution control, large geographical areas and disaster recovery. There are numerous mechanical structures for preserving the efficient reliability of wireless or wired ad hoc networks. Acharya and Asha (2008) have attempted to develop distributed procedures for identifying anomalous activity in data flow configurations in large-scale sensor networks. These algorithms are used as the building blocks for intrusion detection, attack segregation and fully automated reactions for an integrated scheme for ensuring WSN survivability and data flow stability.

WSN machinery is increasingly being utilized for data gathering in Critical Infrastructures (CIs). Coppolino *et al.* (2010) have offered an IDS that is capable of defending a CI from attacks directed at its WSN-based parts. By offering a correct and timely discovery of malicious actions, the projected IDS resolution of this paper ultimately results in a dramatic improvement in terms of security, since chances were given for carrying out suitable remediation/reconfiguration actions that counter the attack and/or let the method allow it. This paper offers elementary concepts, deliberates on the main application problems, and carries out an initial investigation.

2.16 ENERGY-EFFICIENT IDS

Security problems are caused as a result of, firstly, the deployment of minute sensors with restricted battery life in an exposed and insecure environment and, secondly, the dynamic topology in WSNs. One critical security challenge is to identify network intrusion because attacks can happen from any direction and any node in WSNs. Based on diverse WSN routing protocol classifications, in terms of their energy-efficient manner, there are a number of algorithms for building IDSs. Salehian *et al.* (2010) have delivered an overview of the research on IDS in WSNs, concentrating on routing protocol classifications depending on network structure in regard to power utilization as an essential parameter in these types of linkages.

Li *et al.* (2010) have offered an IDS founded on a hierarchical structure in a WSN. The projected structure was simple and enhanced the security of the WSN. A multi-nodule with the idea of joint collaboration and intrusion detection nodules with the anomaly detection algorithm were used in this model. The power consumption can be reduced with the real data from the anticipated algorithm. The key features of the WSN are investigated first in this paper, then the authors express the most common intrusion detection architectures of WSNs, in addition to considering their advantages and disadvantages in detail.

Yu *et al.* (2010) have presented a new situation where the invader can destroy confronted sensors. Using their system model, this condition was evaluated theoretically and experimentally. The intrusion detection issue was debated differently, according to the speed of the attacker. This results in detection possibility, which can be applied to any sensor deployment using the disc model. A single-sensing detection model and a multiple-sensing detection model were also used in the detection model in this paper. This paper also measured some exciting features in ID, for instance, the transmission period, sampling period, and the random entrance time of the invader.

Various security protocols or instruments have been designed for WSNs. The IDS for a conventional network cannot be applied openly in WSNs because of its resource limitations. Several structures have been offered to identify intrusions in WSNs. Yu and Tsai (2008) have organized a framework of machine learning-based IDS for WSNs. The projected system of this paper was not restricted to certain attacks, while the "machine learning algorithm" helped to form a detection system from training data automatically, which prevented the need for human labor to write a signature of attacks or specify the standard behavior of a sensor node.

Abduvaliyev *et al.* (2013) have presented a complete classification of several IDS methods in relation to their employed detection methods. Anomaly detection, misuse detection, and specification-based detection protocols were analyzed in this paper. The authors give an explanation of existing security attacks in WSNs and, in order to challenge those attacks, equivalent protocols were suggested. They also examined works regarding the network structure of WSNs. Moreover, they emphasized numerous serious deficiencies that IDSs presently have and defined future research pathways for IDSs in wireless sensor networks. A few limited surveys on this subject have previously been completed, but the authors felt that there was a great need to perform a thorough and comprehensive study on the vital features of IDS in WSNs. The key feature of this paper was to take in the most recent progressions in this area along with forecasting future studies so that both general and expert readers could benefit.

Traditional IDSs for WSNs only focus their considerations on a specific routing protocol, which lacks universality and flexibility. Guo *et al.* (2015) have projected a universal method – MPOID (Multi-Protocol Oriented Intrusion Detection) – to solve the issue of multi-protocol intrusion detection. Their work can generate all the attack types for any routing protocol of a WSN, some of which, additionally, can be precisely detected with the automatically produced rules. This paper formalized the routing protocol with the Process Algebra for Wireless Mesh Networks (AWN) language. It also categorized all the possible attacks into four types according to four original purposes, and it generated all the attack targets, traces and types.

The neighbor-based detection method of the paper by Stetsko *et al.* (2010) explores the principle that sensor nodules located geographically near to one another are inclined to have related behavior. If the performance of a node significantly varies from its neighbors, then the node is considered as malicious. This detection method was localized, unsupervised and modified in accordance with changing network dynamics. The method was encouraging, but it has not been profoundly investigated in the framework of wireless sensor networks so far. In this paper, the authors also offered indications that can be employed in the neighbor-based method intended for the discovery of selective forwarding, jamming and hello flood assaults. The precision of the method in the detection of selective forwarding, jamming and hello flood assaults was thus assessed in this paper.

The paper of Tseng *et al.* (2015) discusses and performs lab research for discovering the LQI value of the ZigBee wireless sensor network and from the variation of LQI values to determine whether there is any intrusion. While it fluctuates when someone intrudes into the area, it requires a stable LQI value in closed and indoor areas where no one is present. By using the difference in LQI values, an IDS is developed. After the system was authenticated, this paper further established an in-house intrusion monitor system where, once somebody intrudes, the system will sound an alarm or send a message to the cell phone of the owner to warn them that there has been an intrusion in order to achieve the in-house security protection effect.

Multi-level network architecture has proven to be more valuable than single-level network architecture in terms of power efficiency, adaptability, performance and dependability for WMSN applications. The paper by Zhao *et al.* (2012) on a multimedia intrusion detection application seems to be a promising application of multi-level WMSNs, where the lower level can sense the intruder by means of scalar sensors, and the upper level camera nodes are roused to send real time video sequences from the sensed zone. Though energy consumption and network overheads would be reduced, the transmission of multimedia content requires a particular quality level from the user's point of view. Forward Error Correction (FEC) can be considered as a suitable solution from the existing devices for refining video transmissions from the user's point of view. In this work, Zhao *et al.* have projected a Quality of Experience (QoE)-aware FEC mechanism for WMSNs, which generates redundant packets based on the influence of the frame on the user experience.

Existing IDSs work in separation from the access control in WSNs. The lack of cooperation between these mechanisms cannot deliver sufficient security for WSNs. As the paper by Wu (2013) showed, access control depends on usage control (UCON), and the author's method delivered variable qualities and constant access decision. This paper also established an adaptive decision tree construction mechanism for intrusion detection. The proposal of this paper can also guard against standard attacks as well as refined lasting attacks and anomalous attacks on WSNs. The structure of this paper provided an example of the strategy as a way to assess the above.

2.17 CONCLUSION

IDS allows us to recognize undesirable intrusions for wired systems, and thus it assists with the accomplishment of a wide security method. There are distinctive methodologies and techniques to create an intrusion detection system for wired systems, yet a few of their strategies are not reasonable for remote systems. Concealing security objectives from intrusion detection is the task of detection activities in Information Security. Intrusion identification and response to DDoS assaults against the associated computer frameworks is the general point of system security. Moreover, cyber assaults can be created from different locations and, furthermore, can target different machines. Accordingly, a strategy is needed to detect such types of system information. From the existing literature, we have observed that security is the major challenge for WSNs, especially during attacks such as Sybil, DDoS, etc. We now have to propose a technique to solve this issue.

CHAPTER 3

MOTIVATION

3.1 HONEYPOT: INTRUSION DETECTION SYSTEM

The aim of the current work is to introduce honeypots, which secure clients' data and prevent intruders from accessing the framework or the network. The honeypot framework plays a major role in the identification of attackers and establishing them as a malicious source. Honeypots are widely utilized for the prevention and detection of attacks that diminish security measures and convert the framework into a more proficient system for the estimation of security functions. The honeypot utilization mechanism gives security against intruders directly to the systems. Fundamentally, a honeypot is a framework that gathers and gains knowledge about data. The major drawback behind this is that it is not possible to detect the black-hat attackers as well as establish tasks towards them (Tseng *et al.* 2015). Additionally, the major aims are to detect the attackers and hackers as well as to gather information about the hackers. This captured data will be utilized for the upcoming investigations. We are proposing a novel concept known as a virtual honeypot, which recognizes and captures network intrusions.

The proposed work introduces the honeypot framework aided by IDS. These techniques are regarded as the main concepts for defensive functions. This methodology is also regarded as a flexible security mechanism and also prevents information from being stolen by the attackers. The proposed methodology includes major functionalities in order to confuse the attackers as well as to gather the framework's information, and then directs them onto the wrong path. This process distinguishes the attacker's movement with new techniques and applications. The intruders may have a place within the black-hat group, and attempt to take over the information that is stolen from the framework, aided by recent applications like TCP address, IP address, and so on. After gaining information about the attacker's next action, the honeypot framework will protect the user's information and secure it from the attackers. The honeypot framework plays a major role in identifying intruders (Stetsko *et al.* 2010).

3.2 ANT-BASED DDOS TECHNIQUE UTILIZING ROAMING VIRTUAL HONEYPOT

The goal of the proposed work is to maximize the packet delivery proportion, thus reducing the number of packet drops and the false positive outcomes of the attacks. We have introduced the ADTRVH technique, where the virtual roaming honeypot has been utilized and aided by a multi-level protection model in order to group the data with regards to different intruders at various levels in the system. In view of the ACO method, the gathered data is transmitted to several aspects of the security pattern, thus diminishing the number of honeypot intruders as well as avoiding the distribution of intruders (Abduvaliyev *et al.* 2013). The MLIP distinguishes system intruders to various degrees. After the identification of the affected domain, the information is transmitted to various levels in order to eliminate the contiguous distribution of attacks to the honeypot framework by establishing a defense framework over the attackers. This illustrates that the newly introduced methodology diminishes the proportion of packet delivery and minimizes false positives.

Here, we build up a security framework for the establishment of ADTRVH. This methodology actualizes approaches to keep attackers away and protects the honeypot from different frameworks' attacks by diminishing the attack distribution. Subsequently, the intruder is regarded as the contaminator. The honeypot uses the table logs of the IP to a great extent. This may cause congestion if a tremendous number of attacks are sustained (Yu & Tsai 2008). The congestion that goes beyond the limited point is dropped in the last one. Furthermore, an application that relates to various logging degrees is utilized to maintain the attacker's details in the logs of the framework. By the time the attackers hack the honeypot, the framework record ought to be preserved in the current server log. These days, propelled attacks have the ability to interrupt it, which is why the layer with the server log is utilized. In this way, the framework logs' data is held and later attacks the honeypots (Li *et al.* 2010).

3.3 EIDS-BASED HONEYPOT SYSTEM

The aim of the proposed Firecol Protection Base Honeypot System (FPS-HPS) is to decrease system intrusion during the interaction. This study is comprised of an FBS, LB and honeypot framework that enhances the execution of the attack identification framework. The load balancer creates tokens for the licensed client and attackers in terms of Firecol Protection Services outcomes. It maintains a strategic distance from unwanted communication and computation in the Firecol framework and the LB. It additionally reduces the time and expense of the defected data (Solmaz *et al.* 2010).

The motivation behind this examination work is to portray what honeypot frameworks are and illustrate their evaluated results to the system security community. It can be utilized for creation purposes by responding to, detecting and preventing attackers. It can also be utilized for gathering data so they can grasp danger better and prevent attacks.

The intrusions, as well as attacks, will be avoided by utilizing the FPSIDS-HPS approach. This approach has five main parts for handling and avoiding different system intrusions, namely, the FPS, LB, MS, TV and honeypot systems: 1) the original user is initially connected to the Internet and then starts the communication process, with the FPS user status being checked initially and forwarded into the load balancer; 2) the token key is generated by the load balancer for the user and the attacker which attacks the network. Two different token keys are generated by the load balancer with different ranges. The generated token key is forwarded by the load balancer to the mail server; 3) the key is sent to the user separately by the mail server and then it is verified by the token key verifier; 4) the key range is checked by the verifier to identify whether it came from the original user or not. The data are sent to the user by the server after the verification request is received. The token key is sent by the attacker and the token range received is different. The request should be forwarded to the honeypot system; and 5) the irrelevant data are transferred by the attacker to the attacker. A powerful intrusion detection system (IDS) provided by the honeypot was used to determine the intrusion.

3.4 EIDPS: AN EFFICIENT APPROACH TO PROTECT THE NETWORK AND INTRUSION PREVENTION

The aim of the current work is to avoid intrusion attacks on the network. Thus, in order to avoid intrusions, the Enhanced Interruption Detection Prevention System (EIDPS) is proposed. The classification of attackers is done by utilizing the intrusion detection prevention system (IDPS). With the help of the proposed approach, it achieves efficient security throughout the entire network by avoiding unknown third-party attackers.

Our framework gives ongoing security to licensed clients aided by Sebek, Snort and Dionaea. This likewise gives a characterization of attacks by utilizing the SVM specification and, to keep away intruders, malicious code and for the identification of packets, we used an IDPS (Coppolino *et al.* 2010). At that point, a honeypot framework is used to resolve the issue of attackers. In the end, our framework gives efficient security to licensed clients and in addition keeps the system intrusion within the network.

Our proposal introduces a new intrusion identification and preventive framework, referred to as an Enhanced IDPS framework, for responding to, securing, and protecting the framework from intrusion as well as from attackers. Thus, to shield the approved client from attacks, our proposed framework utilizes different applications like Sebek, Snort, Dionaea, SVM, IDPS, and a honeypot server. The introduced framework has two essential elements: the server and the client. Depending upon the client component, Dionaea client, Snort IDS, and Sebek user procedures have been utilized for the evaluation of non-licensed users.

Related to the server element, the Dionaea server, Verifier, and Sebek server procedures have been established for the client to detect individual packets. At that point, the normalization application is implemented to standardize the functions of both the client and the server as well as to evaluate the observations that relate to the attackers. Finally, it directs the detected observations to the fundamental server (Acharya & Asha 2008). The fundamental server contributes two operations: the IDPS and the attack categorization framework. The IDPS recognizes and eliminates the packets transmitted by the malicious client. The attack categorization framework is utilized for the reorganization of the attackers, and it also supports vector machine characterization. The classification framework also includes a new kind of assault. Thus, after detecting the attackers, our honeypot framework sends fake information to the attackers according to the attack type.

3.5 AN EFFICIENT ODAIDS-HPS MECHANISM FOR RESPONDING TO, PREVENTING, AND DETECTING DDoS ATTACKS

The aim of the current work is to determine how to handle the attacks in an efficient way. In order to carry this out, the ODAIDS approach proposes an assault (attack) classifier framework. This extricates the sorts of assaults that efficiently apply dataset components as well as outlier values. In the characterized results, it is shown that nodes assault an efficient system in the proposed honeypot framework.

Our ODAIDS approach documented those categories of successful disruptions after which the interruption features are forwarded to the proposed assault (attack) classifier framework. An assault classifier framework discriminates the sorts of assault that productively operate the dataset components and outlier values (Zhang *et al.* 2009). After that, the characterized result, which is that nodes assault an efficient system, is sent to the proposed honeypot framework. Hereafter, we would outline that an entire intrusion detection framework must extricate and cancel all assaults against entirely computational dangers. Anyway, the proposed framework distinguishes each computational danger compared to a less effective intrusion detection system.

The DDoS assaults are divided into three classifications: the first is the volume-based assaults that incorporate ICMP floods as well as fake packet floods. Second is the protocol assaults, which is wherever a resource of a genuine server is compromised via an assault. This basically incorporates ping of death, STN floods, DDoS floods, and fragmented packet attacks. Third is the zero-day DDoS assault, which is a moderate collision of the network server. DDoS assaults can be avoided by means of utilizing the proposed ODAIDS-HPS framework.

The proposed network framework structure comprises three imperative parts that are conveyed to protect against DDoS assaults, which are the outlier detection-based IDS, the attack classifier and the honeypot system (Vamsi & Kant 2015). Original servers should be received in an approved client utilizing legitimate data by means of an ODA-based IDS. The attacker's agent overflows the actual server, and subsequently the operators are framework or software mechanisms. The actual server's resources are possessed by operators with the aid of malicious data.

CHAPTER 4

HONEYPOT TECHNIQUE FOR INTRUSION DETECTION

4.1 INTRODUCTION TO INTRUSION DETECTION

The most important area in information technology (IT) is computer system security. Progress is very quick in this field because information should be secure and should not be leaked to attackers by the compression of data and intrusion (Idowu *et al.* 2013). All over the world, the internet has become a popular technique to communicate with computers. Some new possibilities for users to be affected by malicious activity have been created by the constancy of communication. Over the network the significance of security is growing, and the IDS is one of the methods used to identify the behavior of malicious users (Jabez & Muthukumar 2015). Every day, the number of internet users is increasing. Crowd-based internet traffic is getting higher, so internet security is required mostly in the area of computing networks.

The revolution of networking has finally come of age in the past few years. Computation can be changed by the internet in ways that have never been known before. The chances of malicious intrusions are provided by limitless possibilities.

The mechanisms of the security of a system are designed by system resources and data for the prevention of unauthorized access. At present, security does not appear to be completely preventative and is unrealistic. When attempts of intrusion are detected, attempts are made to repair the damage and some action may be taken.

In the likely event of unauthorized intrusion, the intruder will attempt to:

- Access information
- Control information
- Render the system unusable

4.2 NECESSITY OF INTRUSION DETECTION SYSTEMS

Due to the increase in connectivity on the internet, the computer system provides integrity, confidentiality and assurance against denial of service. In the bigger picture, there are financial possibilities that open up systems and render them vulnerable to attacks by intruders. In the operating system, the subversion attempts to exploit flaws and application programs, and this results in spectacular incidents.

The attempts at intrusion are categorized in two ways. In order to prevent the intrusion itself, a completely secure system is built. For instance, all users are required to authenticate and identify themselves, and, by using various methods of cryptography, the data are protected and access to them is controlled by mechanisms.

1. Building completely secure systems is not possible in practice. Programs report bugs and operating systems indicate bug-free software. The design and implementation of a totally secure system is difficult.
2. The cryptographic method has its own problems. Passwords can be cracked and lost, and the user's password and crypto-systems can be broken entirely.
3. The security system is vulnerable to abuse by insiders whose privileges are abused.
4. The relationship level between the access, control and efficiency of a user is inversed; when mechanisms are strict, there is less efficiency.

If the attacks have been detected in the system in real time, appropriate action is taken immediately. The intrusion detection does not take any preventive measure if the attack is detected normally and, rather than being a pro-active agent, it is reactive, which makes the role of an informant important.

The intrusion is detected by audit data by the operating system. Audit trail activities for the system are recorded, and files are logged in chronological order. Activities are logged on the system, and the logs may be used for a manual inspection of intrusion detection.

4.3 OVERVIEW OF PROPOSED WORK

Honeypots are used as traps in the field of security, prevention and detection; where security measures abound, measurements are more efficient and accurate. In security systems, the honeypot consumption method implements the honeypot's role. Basically, the honeypot mechanism is designed to collect and learn information. Catching the attacker from the black-hat group is not the main aim, and it also puts the focus on attacker attraction and hacker information collection. This information will be helpful for further ideas and studies on attacking. The novel idea of the virtual honeypot identifies intrusions on the network.

4.4 INTRUSION DETECTION

4.4.1 Network-Based Intrusion Detection System

The network-based intrusion detection system (NIDS) detects the mass flow that ended the host of another. The size of the area based on the intrusion will be observed in the network as an increase or decrease. The network has capability against the crowd over a network in order to maintain the effect based on the system of intrusion detection. With high traffic, NIDS have to make traffic clear and observable in time. NIDS are placed at strategic points in the network to monitor traffic to and from all devices within the network. The passing traffic analysis is matched to the known attacks library on the entire subnet. Once the attack identification has been made, then the abnormal behavior is sensed and an alert is sent to the administrator. NIDS would then be installed on a subnet where firewalls are located in order to monitor for breaks through the firewall. The inbound and outbound traffic can be scanned accurately, however a bottleneck is created which impairs the network's overall speed. The network is observed in real time by on-line NIDS, the ethernet packets are analyzed, and some rules are applied to decide whether an attack has been found or not. To discover if the attack is present or not, the off-line NIDS deals with stored data and goes through some processes.

4.4.2 Host Intrusion Detection System

In the network itself, an individual host or device is used in the host intrusion detection system (HIDS). The inbound and outbound packets are monitored by the HIDS from the device, and the consumer alerts the administrator if any unusual activity is noticed. The alert will be sent to the administrator to investigate if any system files have been modified or deleted. For example, the usage of HIDS can be perceived in any change in the function of a critical machine that was not anticipated to make configuration changes. The intrusion system can be used particularly by means of the custom tools and the honeypot.

4.4.3 Anomaly-based Intrusion Detection System

The detection of anomalies assumes intrusive activities. For a system, normal activity profiles can be established by anomaly detection. All system conditions vary from profile to profile, which are established statistical amounts of intrusion attempts. A set of intrusive activities only interconnects anomalous activities in the exact same place. There are two interesting possibilities:

- If the anomalous activities are not intrusive then they are flagged as intrusive;
- If the intrusive activities are not anomalous, the result is a false negative and the intrusion is not flagged. This problem is more serious than the false positive problem and is a very dangerous one.

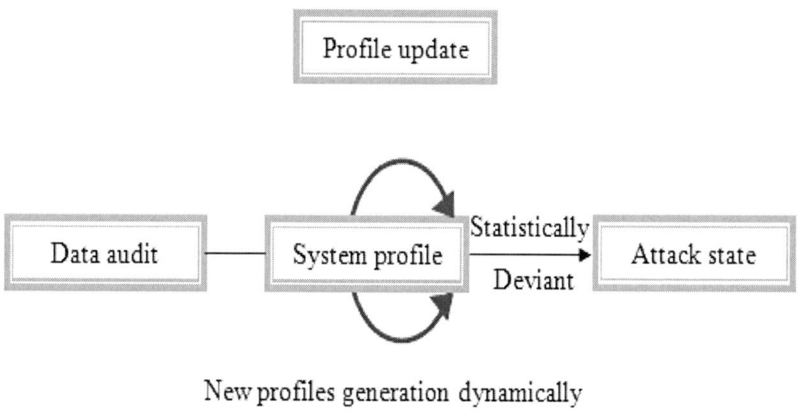

Figure 4.1: Anomaly-based detection system

In the anomaly detection system, the level of threshold selection becomes a major issue and solves the problem with anomalous activities and intrusive activities and monitors the feature selection. Using the anomaly-based intrusion detection system, the transaction, behavior, activity and outgoing traffic are observed. Users' behavior is checked on the supposition that they are varying from their normal behavior and they are subsequently identified as an attacker. The system administrator sets the normal behavior limitations. AIDS causes a heavy burden on a network system. There are two types of anomalies: false positives and false negatives. If anomalies are flagged as intrusive when they are not, they are identified as false positives, and anomalies are false negatives if they are not flagged as intrusive when they are.

4.4.4 Misuse Detection

The misuse detection scheme has the ability to represent attacks in a pattern or signature form, so variations of the same attack will take place.

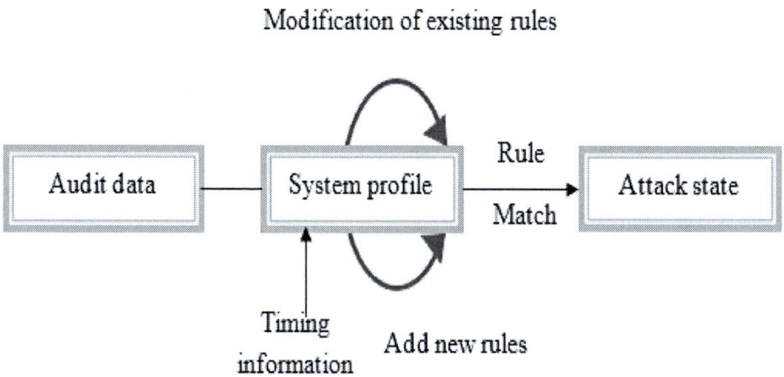

Figure 4.2: Misuse detection system

All the patterns of attack are detected by the virus detection systems. There will be very little usage for methods of an unknown attack. The anomaly detection system is used for the detection of complements of bad behavior, which is an interesting point to note. The bad behavior is recognized by the misuse detection system. The main issues in misuse detection are writing a signature that encompasses a pertinent attack variation, and signatures that do not match the non-intrusive activity. There are different methods used in misuse detection, including new pattern matching.

4.5 HONEYPOT

When imitating the honeypot system in intrusion detection, there was a tendency for the intruder to break the limit in overall network access. Unknown attackers are tricked and monitored. Inside the firewall, the honeypot system was installed to control the full network; however, implementation is also possible outside of the firewall. An opposite firewall system within the honeypot allows the incoming attackers in instead of blocking them and the path gets diverted from a real to a false database, and the function the attacker is trying to access is restricted.

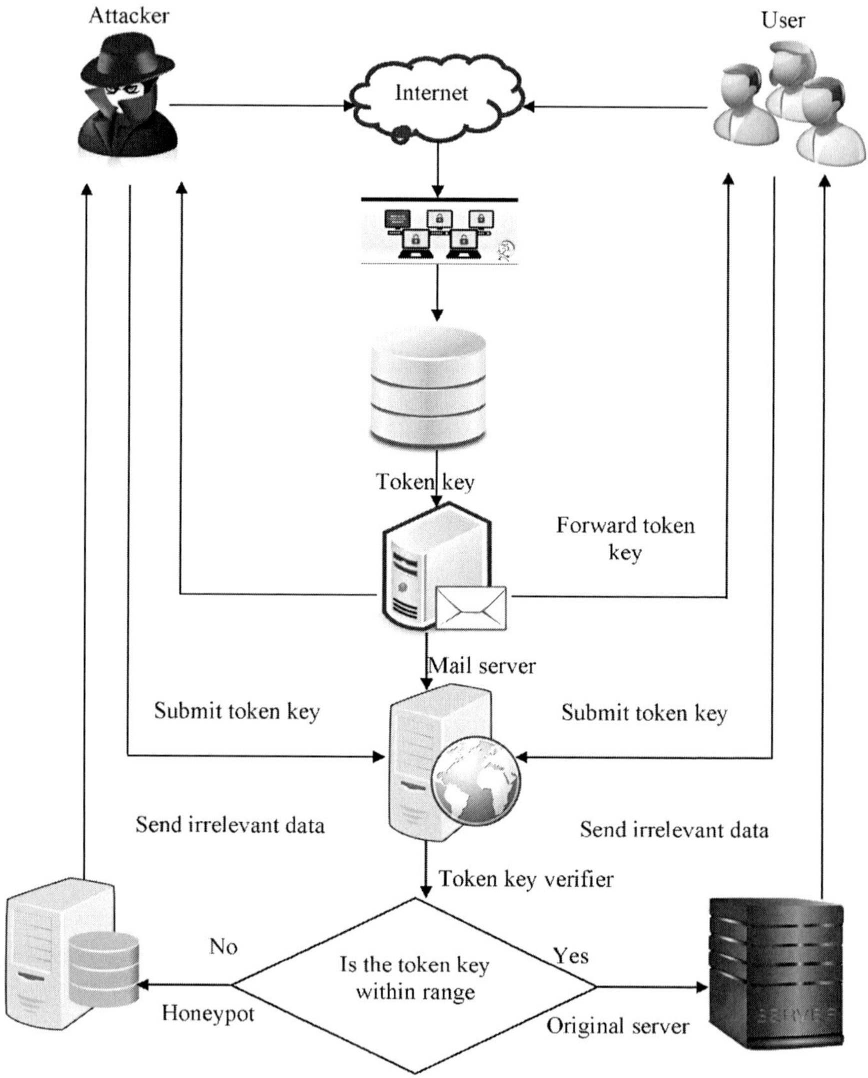

Figure 4.3: Proposed honeypot architecture

The honeypot is developed and analyzed in the network for the detection of malicious attacks. For the honeypot attackers, the machine appears to be an actual database, server and OS. Attackers are attracted by the honeypot system and attacks are invited. The honeypot is secure from the attacker, and information is gained by the creation of log events of unsafe activity from a particular IP (Maleh *et al.* 2015). The zombie machine that the attackers have control over performs in an automated and well-organized environment, for which the network enterprise is preferable. In the cyber-attack, the systems that are infected are more dangerous and are decontaminated with Active Cyber Defense (ACD). The scalable effect and practical system withstand growth ability, and malware identification is efficient for detecting infected machines (Sun *et al.* 2013).

The honeypot's main aim is to identify the attacker, access the network and store information (TCP address, IP address, etc.) about the intrusion. Instead of the real database, the access path is diverted to the fake database. Intrusion detection is a major problem for research behavior (Wang *et al.* 2013). Attackers' identification and the capture of the intruder's information are based on knowledge of the black-hat group and intelligence. Honeypots' behavior is one of the most important agents for this.

Services based on signatures include IDS and firewalls in signature-based detection fields with more ideas. The honeypot is one of the most interesting techniques for controlling attacks on the internet. Information about the attacker can be collected easily. The risk of attacks can be reduced more by the honeypot than by other techniques (Sajjad *et al.* 2015). Valuable data are collected easily from all systems once an attacker has breached the firewall and nothing remains to be saved (Dhakne & Chatur 2015). There is a possibility for the system to prevent booby traps and intruders attacking the system with additional approaches. Information about the attacker is collected by the interaction of the system with the attacker, which is called the honeypot.

4.6 PACKET ANALYSIS

A packet analysis is conducted for packet capturing and information exploration. The information consists of the IP, TCP, UDP header and ICMP. A division of the packet between two sources and the destination IP address for four seconds of record storage takes place. In every connection, the functionality defines the normal attack behavior. The analysis of the packet is designed to identify problems of the network in resolving issues like connectivity loss, DNS issues, sluggish speed and malware infection.

4.7 SVM

SVM design is a classifier that classifies the binary format. The multi-class application solves problems of classification. The SVM is supported by the decision tree. The decision tree and SVM get combined to improve ways to solve multi-class problems. The SVM is effective; the timing of the testing and training processes can be reduced, and the efficiency of the system gets increased. The datasets are divided into several subsets. There are some distinct ways to create a binary tree from root to leaf until all subsets are merged into one class. The binary tree construction function has a massive range of power for classification.

The universal constructive learning procedure has a support vector machine based on statistical learning theory. The SVM is used for two groups of classification problems. The input vectors are linearly mapped to a very high-dimensional feature space. The linear decision surface is constructed in the feature space.

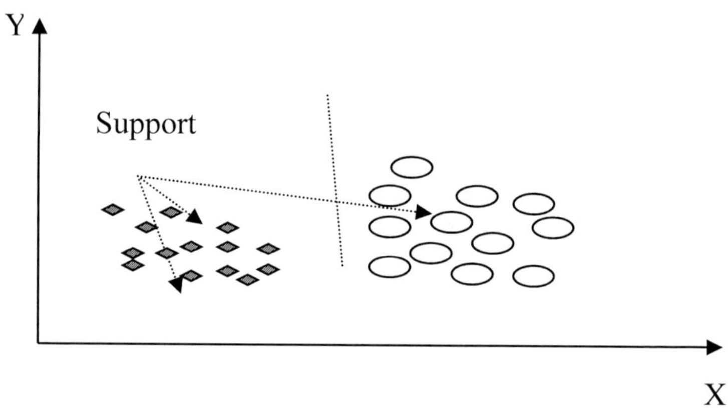

Figure 4.4: Support vectors in SVM

For linear two-class classifications with SVM, the margin of minimum distance indicates the margin from the hyperplane separation to the closest data points. The learning machine of SVM seeks an optimal hyperplane separation at a high margin. The important and unique approach is based on the solution of data points. These points are known as support vectors.

4.7.1 Identify the right hyperplane

There are three hyperplanes that segregate the classes. Maximizing the nearest data point's distance from the right hyperplane will decide the right hyperplane. This distance is called the margin.

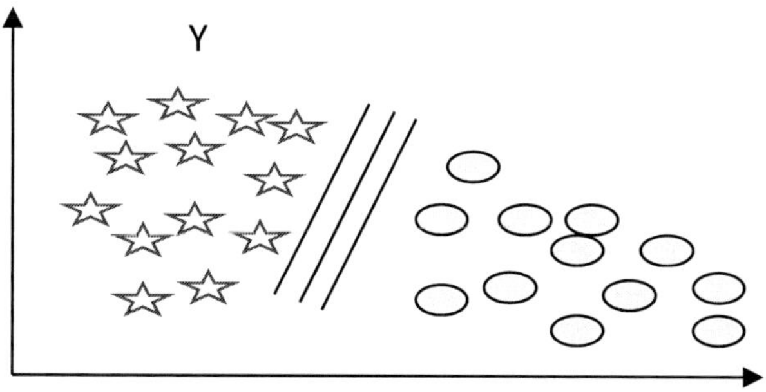

Figure 4.5: Identification of the right hyperplane

4.7.2 Classification into two classes

There is a feature of SVM which is to ignore outliers and find the hyperplane which has the maximum margin. Hence, SVM is robust to outliers.

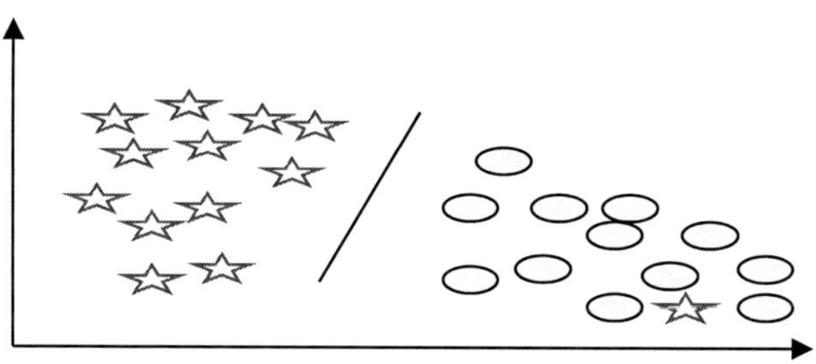

Figure 4.6: classification into two classes

4.8 IDS ALGORITHM

4.8.1 Intrusion Detection System

The packets are taken from the network as the input for the intrusion detection system and the incoming flow time slot is monitored. At this time of slot process and packet monitoring, the malicious time slot is detected by the intrusion detection system and the suspicious flow is checked; the malicious flow was attracted from the traffic, and the new filtering rule is processed and generated. For intrusion detection, signatures are built from the filtering rule:

$$IDS(T,P)=\{L2,\ FR,SGN\}$$

T represents the time slot

$L2$ indicates the log report

FR represents the filtering rule

SGN denotes the signature created

Honeypots can be categorized as pure, high-interaction and low-interaction honeypots.

The production systems which are fully-fledged are pure honeypots. The activities of production systems that host various services are imitated by the high-interaction honeypots, and lots of services are provided to the attacker, which may lead to them wasting their time. Multiple honeypots can be hosted on a single physical machine, which is then used as a virtual machine.

The packets which are captured are used as inputs for the honeypot, and it proceeds to get system information from the packets' origin (Selvaraj, Kuthadi and Marwala 2016). The honeypot precedes the packet analysis and generates replies to involve the client from the host.

$HP_i(P_i) = L_i1 + CLD_i$

$P_i = \{ UDP_i, TCP_i, ICMP_i \}$

$UDP_i, TCP_i, ICMP_i$ = packet sets

$CLD_i = \{ P_i \text{ Type}, P_i \text{ Reply}, cIP_i \}$= client information

cIP_i = client IP_i

P_i = type of packet

P_i Reply = packet reply

L_i1 = report log

4.8.2 Packet Analysis

- **Algorithm**

1. Start receiving packet

   For each packet p

   if (received_protocol = Transmission Control Protocol)

   Infer features of Transmission Control Protocol extract

   else

   if (received_protocol = User Datagram Protocol)

   Infer features of User Datagram Protocol

   Else

   if (received_protcol = Internet Control Message Protocol)

   Infer features of Internet Control Message Protocol

2. Wait for two seconds after feature collection
3. Based on two Internet Protocol addresses' connection, split the data into records.
4. Apply DT rules for all connections
5. Log output
6. End

4.9 RESULTS AND DISCUSSION

Datasets were extracted for the measurement of the performance in the proposed approach. Table 4.1 shows all the existing techniques. The honeypot finds the identification of the intrusion and the honeypot detection rate is high among them. Overall, the honeypot intrusion detection rate is high for all 12 features.

The honeypot is the most effective and efficient method in comparison with other existing techniques. The experiment results present a comparison between honeypots and some existing techniques where irrelevant information gets produced. Table 4.1 shows the performance analysis for normal and DoS intrusions.

Table 4.1: Classifiers and accuracy after intrusion

Features used	Classifier	Accuracy	Normal		DoS	
			True Positive	False Positive	True Positive	False Positive
12	OneR	82.625	0.895	1.001	0.811	0.213
12	C4.5	91.795	0.937	0.106	0.876	0.118
12	Naïve bayes	81.443	0.854	0.059	0.806	0.105
12	Honey pot	97.953	0.999	0.003	0.979	0.001

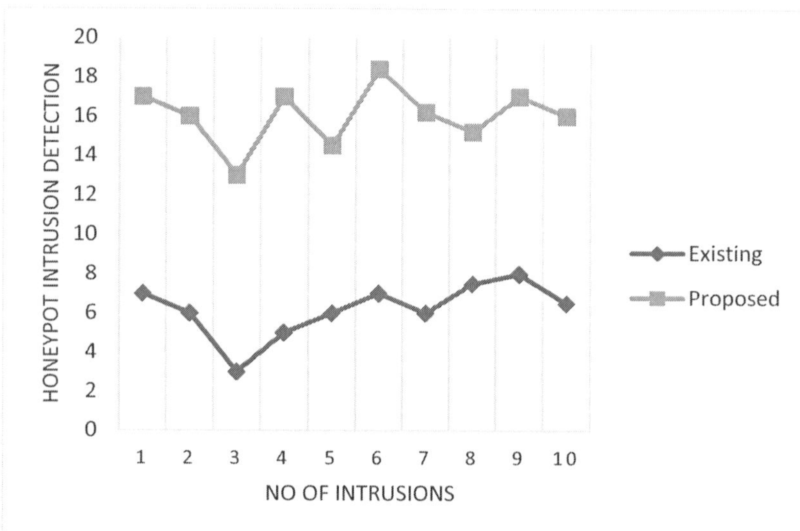

Figure 4.7: Honeypot intrusion detection system

Figure 4.7 shows the detection rate of the honeypot system, which is high compared to existing techniques.

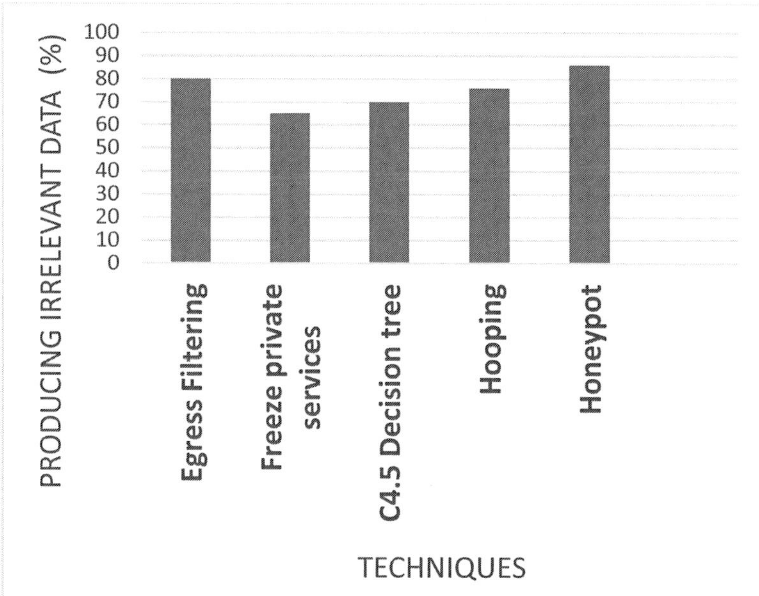

Figure 4.8: Irrelevant information production for attackers

The percentages of irrelevant information produced for attackers by different techniques are given in Figure 4.8. More irrelevant information is produced for attackers or intruders when using the honeypot technique. The honeypot is the best technique to gain information about them.

Table 4.2: Comparisons of delay, packet delivery ratio, and packet drop with existing methods

No of intrusions	Delay		Packet Delivery Ratio		Packet Drop	
	Proposed	Existing	Proposed	Existing	Proposed	Existing
20	7.247	13.075	0.998	0.184	38	21432
40	4.372	5.099	0.997	0.055	58	8456
60	8.152	14.405	0.995	0.107	73	8656
80	7.103	8.858	0.995	0.089	75	9301
100	9.900	10.253	0.991	0.069	122	10276

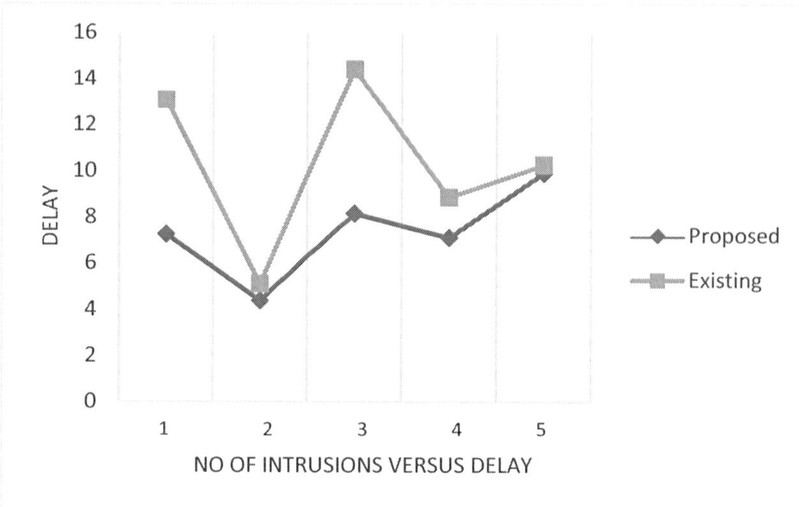

Figure 4.9: No.of intrusions versus delay

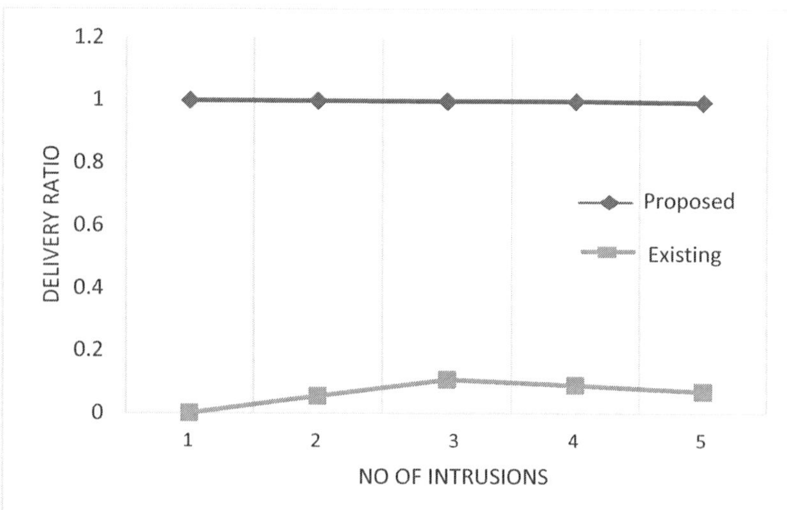

Figure 4.10: No. of intrusions versus delivery ratio

Figure 4.9 represents the number of intrusions versus delay and Figure 4.10 shows the number of intrusions versus the delivery ratio. The overall delay is found out during the transmission of the packet. The delay is less in the proposed system compared to the existing technique. The delivery ratio is higher in terms of the ratio of the received number of packets and the transmission of the total number of packets. The delivery ratio of the proposed technique is higher compared to the existing technique.

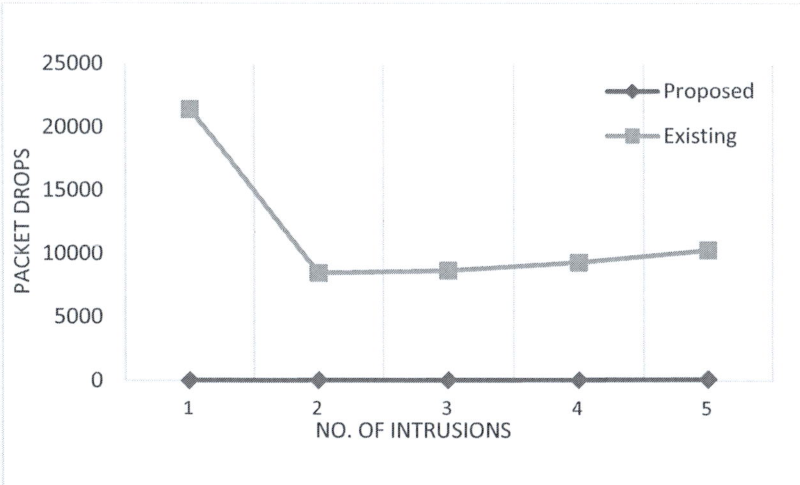

Figure 4.11: Number of intrusions versus packet drops

The number of intrusions versus packet drops is shown in Figure 4.11. Packet drops are the number of packets dropped due to attacker nodes. The number of packet drops occurring in the proposed system is much less compared to the existing technique. As shown in Figure 4.11, the existing technique has a high packet drop level.

Table 4.3 includes the values of residual energy (J), overhead and throughput (packets). A comparison is made for the existing and proposed systems and shows that the proposed system is best.

Table 4.3: Residual energy, overhead and throughput comparisons

No. of intrusion	Residual Energy		Overhead		Throughput	
	Proposed	Existing	Proposed	Existing	Proposed	Existing
20	23947	4.672	11703	18700	0.162	0.0004
40	24035	5.1022	12023	26987	0.3412	0.0004
60	23385	5.733	12343	24478	0.329	0.0107
80	23129	5.464	12663	23856	0.354	0.0141
100	22848	5.128	12983	26857	0.284	0.0269

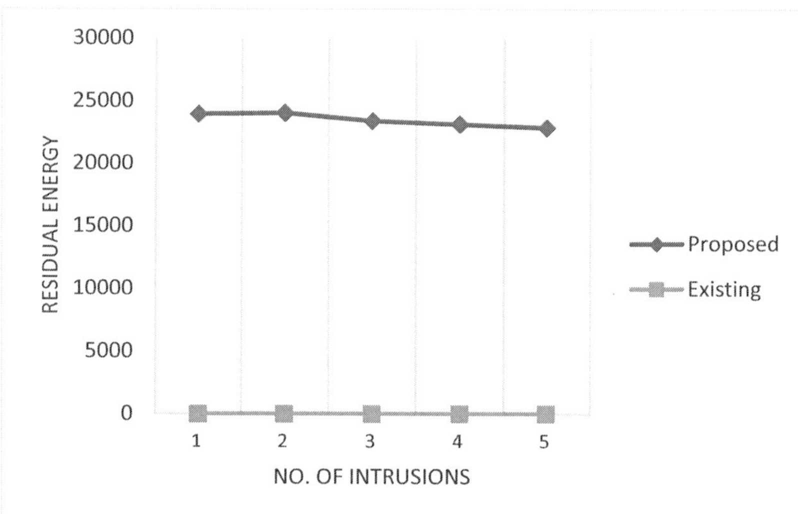

Figure 4.12: No. of intrusions versus residual energy

Figure 4.12 shows the number of intrusions versus residual energy. The residual energy is the energy present in each node. Each node has maximum residual energy compared to the existing system.

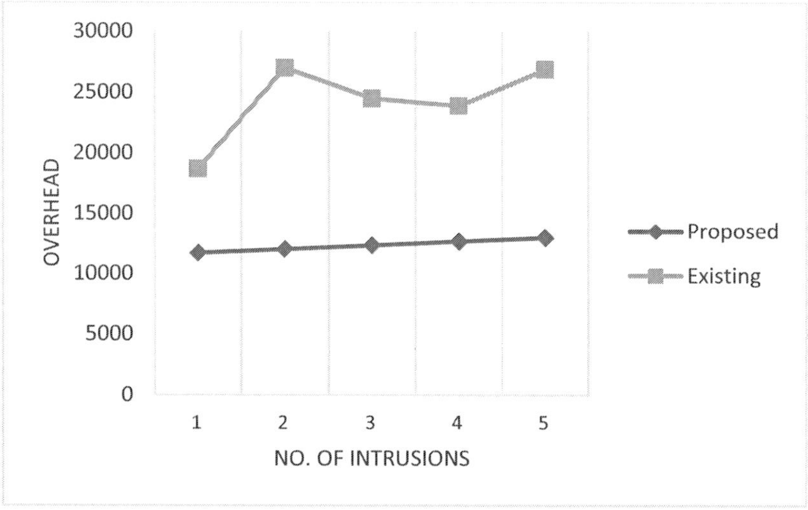

Figure 4.13: No. of intrusions versus overhead

The number of intrusions versus overhead is plotted in Figure 4.13. The overheads of the proposed system are less compared to the existing technique. Figure 4.14 shows the number of intrusions versus throughput. The throughput obtained in the proposed system is higher, which suggests that the proposed technique is more efficient and effective.

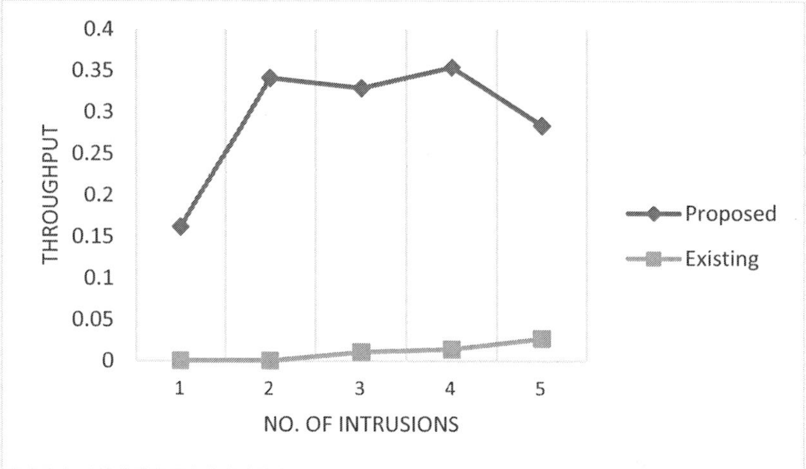

Figure 4.14: No. of intrusions versus throughput

4.10 CONCLUSION

The novel technique proposed here is the honeypot and IDS. This technique plays a major role in the defensive operation of the honeypot. Its methods are very efficient in the network for security purposes, and the stealing of data by attackers or intruders is prevented. The proposed technique confuses the intruders, whose information is collected in the system and who are given wrong paths showing irrelevant data. The proposed technique's novel idea helps to identify the attacker's movement. The new techniques of attackers belonging to the black-hat community tend to steal data from any system, so the information obtained about them, such as their IP and TCP addresses, will help for further work. By knowing the attacker's movement in the honeypot system, the user's information gets secured on the network and intruder access to the system is prevented. The honeypot system plays an important role in the detection of attackers, and it shows them a fake database.

CHAPTER 5

DDoS DETECTION BASED ON THE ANT TECHNIQUE USING ROAMING VIRTUAL HONEYPOTS

5.1 INTRODUCTION

Distributed Denial of Service (DDoS) is a type of network attack. DDoS attacks are one of the most critical security attacks as they threaten network stability (Liu & Yu 2008). The DDoS attack gets relayed to the distributed area, where there are large-scale collaborative attacks aimed at the denial of service.

The one-to-one attack is a DoS attack and aims to lower the configuration of the target computer or reduce the bandwidth of the network. In network technology, DoS attacks are not effective due to rapid growth. The traditional one-way attack was replaced by the DDoS attack with the help of the network, where the puppet machines are continuously mobilized in large numbers by the host in the target destination, so the attack's effect is extremely high (Zhao & Liu 2011). The resource symmetry between the network and the victim is exploited hugely by DoS. In the many-to-one dimension of attack, the network victim is blocked by DDoS, and therefore its level of defense becomes irrelevant (Sandhya & Julian 2014).

The packets are flooded in large numbers and the DDoS attack is launched to overwhelm the victim with multiple compromised hosts, and dispersion in the network takes place. There is a significant flow of attack and the bandwidth of the target system is consumed, or the service of key provisions prevents legitimate users from accessing unauthorized services and thereby posing a major security threat to users on the network. The attack platform is a Botnet, in which DDoS flooding attacks are formed on a large scale. The attack flows are more harmful and distributed, making it hard to increase detection effectively (Rong *et al.* 2011; Coppolino *et al.* 2013; Vamsi & Kant 2015).

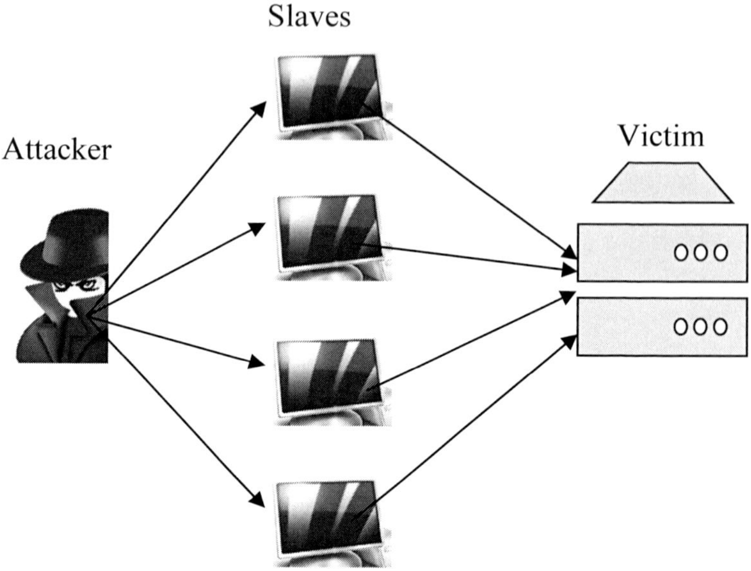

Figure 5.1: A DDoS Attack

5.1.1 Working of a DDoS Attack

The devices connected to the network are taken over by someone who tells the connection to try and send data to a server continuously. More connections can be made by the device to the host of the website and, in order to provide resources for this, the site struggles a lot with legitimate web traffic. During this struggle, the site will load more slowly or go completely offline.

There is irony in a denial of service attack if the users are legitimate and access to the site is not as they regularly expect, as they will reconnect to the site. The attack is magnified by the user through multiple, repeated connections. The attacker also makes repeated connections. This requires the site to use up more resources.

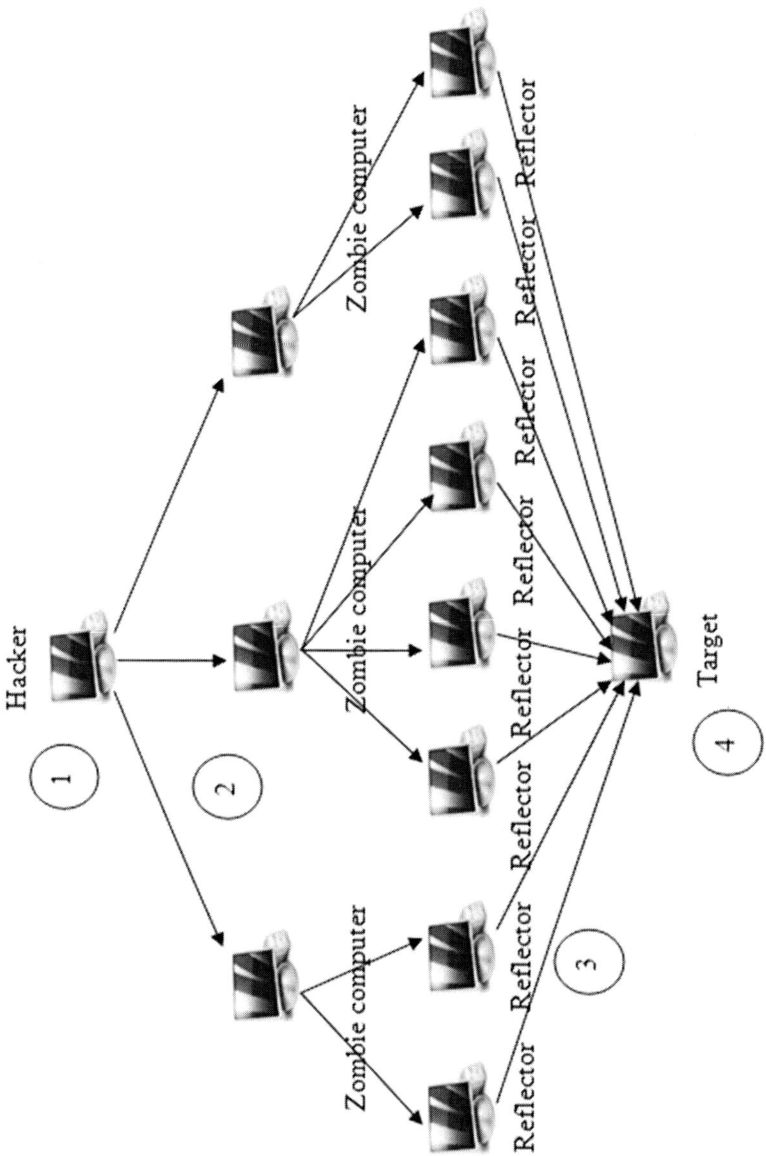

Figure 5.2: Working of a DDoS Attack

Nowadays, an internet site is pretty resilient to single-device service denials. Devices that are connected over the internet are collected by the attacker to send the connection, and they are collectively known as a Botnet. To shut down the Botnet is more difficult when the work is carried out by multiple machines, even though their orders may only be controlled by a single machine. An attacker may rent a Botnet, and vulnerable computers are infected and known as zombies.

5.1.2 DDoS Attacks Detection

The attack stage of DDoS is a hierarchical attack, and tracing attackers is made more difficult by IP spoofing (Zhang *et al.* 2009). DoS migration is hard in a distributed environment as it may be any form of death ping or clone attack. The DDoS state detection algorithm considers that the infrastructure for locating the detection is near the link which is saturated in the victim's vicinity, which makes detection easier. The algorithm simplifies detection response in ineffective circumstances where the available bandwidth has already been consumed on an upstream path (Acharya & Asha 2008).

In DDoS attack detection, on the other hand, packets are transmitted in large numbers; more time is required to analyze each incoming packet, and therefore the accuracy of DDoS detection decreases (Coppolino *et al.* 2010).

5.1.3 Surviving DDoS Attacks

In surviving the DDoS attack, the core router passes the packet to the border router. The router which handles Internet backbone traffic is called the core router. The border router connects the network with the Internet. The core router's owners are contacted through a telecoms company or internet service provider, and they are informed of the problem. The source is contacted to determine the reaching point of malicious traffic in the network.

To reduce the attack temporarily and to reduce the DDoS flood, a few steps are followed. For a single machine, a small change can be made to the IP address to end the flood. The updating of a new address is done on the internal DNS server, and the updated new address is given to the external user. This technique is used for key servers under attack in the network.

5.2 ROLE OF THE HONEYPOT IN THE DETECTION OF A DDoS ATTACK

The resource that will carry out the exchange of information with the intruders is the honeypot. The valuable honeypot is used to provide the exchange of information; it is just used as an administrator, and the information is not modified (Solmaz *et al.* 2010).

A honeypot is an effective tool to provide insights into new attacks and to examine the trends exploited (Li *et al.* 2010). It is a promising approach to obtain attack signatures accurately, and the machines, whether virtual or physical, can detect worm signatures effectively (Yu & Tsai 2008).

Honeypot resources appear to be accessed easily through a non-hardened OS or several vulnerabilities. Similarly to production servers, a decoy system should be set up along with numerous files comprising directories, fake data and loads of other information. By using proper files, the honeypot appears to make the machine legitimate and to make the hacker believe he has access to important information. In order to trap attackers or intruders, the honeypot provides an environment in which to access the attack with actual effects (Abduvaliyev *et al.* 2013).

The intruder penetrates the system normally and the logging-in information is verified by the administrator, who checks the system changes made by the intruder and whether a backdoor to the system is left open. The credibility of the information in the system log record at this point is not high if the administrator is passive.

The honeypot technology improves the speed of detection and response capabilities, the criminal intruder's evidence is collected efficiently, and a good tracking environment is provided. The roaming honeypot scheme assigns servers that activate randomly at precise times. Honeypot servers use the honeypot's location within replica server pools. In a pool, each group of servers with legitimate clients and peer replicas acts as a honeypot for specific time intervals. The roaming of the active server's identification makes it harder for the attackers, who are thus trapped by the honeypots (Stetsko *et al.* 2010).

The drawbacks of traditional honeypots are found in two main areas. These are as follows:

(1) Honeypots can only attack against surveillance and analysis. The intrusion detection system is not supported by bypass listening to monitor the entire network.
(2) The technology of protection honeypots cannot be directly vulnerable to the information system and create a security risk for attackers to exploit.

5.3 PROPOSED SOLUTION

5.3.1. Problem Identification and Overview

The DDoS detection technique is an ant-based technique using roaming virtual honeypots. Due to security attacks like DDoS threatening the internet, system security is essential for safe communication. In order to fool intruders while using a honeypot, an intrusion detection system is implemented, which keeps them far away from reliable distributed network communication.

An efficient hop-by-hop honeypot mechanism is proposed by Zhao *et al.* (2012) to mitigate the spoofing distributed DoS attacks. Backpropagation is performed to trace the root of the attacks. Accurate attack signatures are provided by the roaming honeypots. The roaming honeypot, on receiving attack packets, triggers the activation of a tree of rooted honeypots towards the source attack. Progressive backpropagation is used to handle low rate attacks, which reduces the delay for attacks with a short burst rate, such as on-off attacks.

There is no security system present to protect honeypots from false negatives, unknown attacks, false positives, etc. If an attacker breaks into a honeypot, it will break the connection, which makes it a bouncer. High security is added to the system, and the Ant Colony Optimization (ACO) algorithm is used to trace the intruders' tracks during the detection of the intrusion (Guerroumi *et al.* 2015). If a valuable route is found by the attackers, then the same routes are often used. By tracing their tracks, after detecting the intrusion, attackers' tracks can be stored in the honeypot.

The security system for the architecture has been developed to solve the problem of attackers attacking the honeypot. In the proposed architecture, two technologies were implemented for preventing attackers from making the honeypot attack other systems by controlling the connection and the spread of the attacks (Sun & Liu 2013). As an infected honeypot makes a lot of logs in the IP table, a worm can be detected, and it is automatically blocked after reaching its limit. Traffic exceeding the limit is also dropped. In system logs, in order to protect the attackers' information, a multi-level logging mechanism is used. If the honeypot is hacked by the attacker, a system log will be saved in the remote log server. Nowadays, attacks can be carried out by advanced attackers, so a sniffer server, which is the second layer, is used. The information of the system log is retained after the honeypot is attacked.

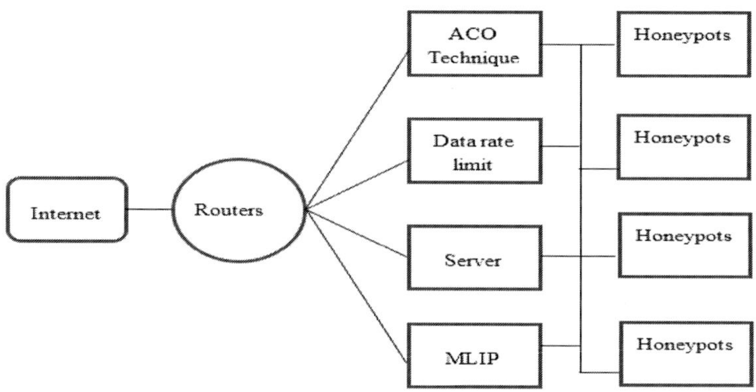

Figure 5.3: Proposed DDoS Defense System

5.3.2 Roaming Virtual Honeypot Process

The hop-by-hop honeypot technique is used to defend against DDoS spoofing for our proposed approach. The hop-by-hop technique starts at the router that is next to the victim of the attack, and the neighboring routers upstream of the attack paths are identified with the help of the packets' attack signature. The process continues until the area of the victim is reached. The server S performs a dual action, which acts as a honeypot on timing factor ρ and as an alternative server to the service provider, in the backpropagation method. Once it is scheduled to be inactive, each server enters a honeypot epoch.

During a honeypot epoch, server S assumes that there is no reasonable traffic. For server S, any packet directed at it is most likely an attack packet. Once server S regains its active condition, the honeypot epoch ends. The honeypot epochs are selected to avoid the interruption of services based on the coordination of server S and receiver R.

The time windows are honeypot epochs in which pure attack packets are received by the server. The intruders that are different are identified, the area affected is kept on record, and the ACO technique is used.

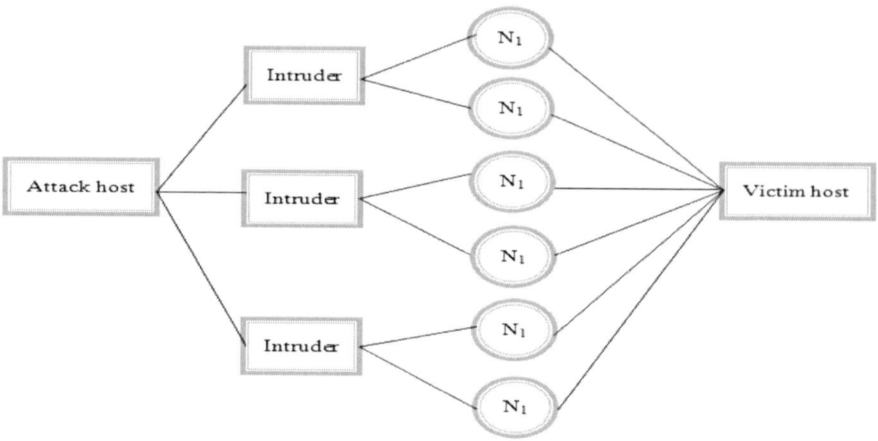

Figure 5.4: Representation of DDoS attack

The backpropagation method of the honeypot is supported by the ACO technique. During the track module, intruders are detected based on pheromone density in the proposed technique, then a report analysis is made and a honeypot is sent to defend the affected area.

5.3.3. ACO

This section describes the ACO technique, which is used to track information about the attackers and maintain various information about misuse, susceptive intrusion and normal access. There are different components used in the ACO, which are detailed in the next subsections.

5.3.3.1 Intrusion Detection Module

Using the intrusion detection module, the unwanted action of the intrusion can be detected. The intrusion detection module observes a system or network for mischievous activities or policy violations. The detected activity or violation is reported to an administrator or collected centrally using the SIEM system. The SIEM system combines outputs from multiple sources, and the technique of alarm filtering is used to distinguish malicious activity from false alarms.

5.3.3.2 Track Module

This module tracks information about different intruders and maintains records of all unwanted actions, such as misuse, normal access and susceptive intrusion. Even the full path and traverse of each distance access, including illegal intrusion and legal access, get tracked and are deposited with different pheromones and module weights.

5.3.3.3 Analysis Module

To keep a record of the attackers, an analysis of the information is made and is transferred to the honeypot.

5.3.4 Introduction of Ant Colony Optimization (ACO)

Using studies done on the complex social behavior of ants and which use the behavioral patterns of ants, scientists are finding models for solving difficult combinatorial optimization problems. With algorithms developed from ant behavior, the ability to find the shortest path has fallen within the field of ACO. ACO is a derivative of Swarm Intelligence (SI). Discrete optimization problems are targeted by the ACO, and continuous optimization problems are extended and are helpful to find approximate solutions. Based on the behavior of ants, the ACO algorithm is the most successful and widely recognized algorithm.

In practice, at the initial stage, the ant walks randomly. Once food is found, the ant returns back to the colony based on past trails where pheromones have been deposited. Hence, the path is easily found by the remaining ants and they follow the track instead of randomly walking. Evaporation starts to occur with the deposited pheromone. This can decrease the attraction. Intrusion navigation is a new field but very similar to the process of ants finding food. Most of them will visit again and again if the intruder finds something important.

- Ants lay a pheromone trail between the nest and food;
- An obstacle interrupts the trail;
- To go around the obstacle, ants find two paths;
- A new pheromone trail is formed along the shorter path.

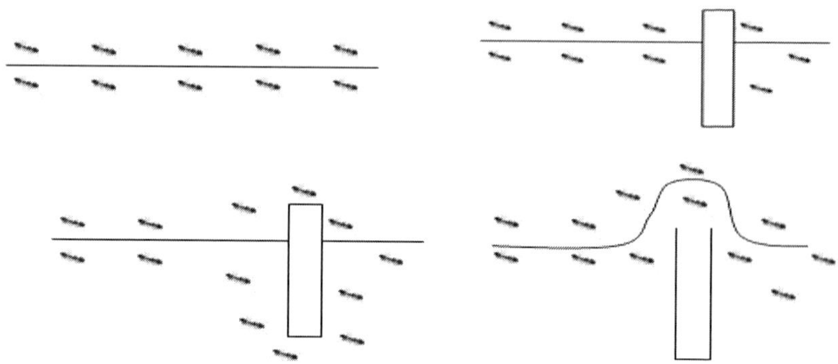

Figure 5.5: Ant behavior

5.3.5 ACO Characteristics

Ant colony optimization characteristics include versatility, robustness and the population-based approach.

5.3.5.1 Versatility

The ACO adapts to the same problems of similar versions: for example, the straightforward extension from TSP to ATSP.

5.3.5.2 Robustness

This is applied in optimization problems of combinatorial reduction such as JSP and QAP.

5.3.5.3 Population-based approach

The exploitation of positive feedback is allowed as a search mechanism, and it is an interesting factor. The implementations made in parallel make the system amenable. In the ACO class of algorithms, the ant system is the first member. The laying of a trail and ants' behavior inspired the algorithm. The essential trait of the ACO algorithm is the combination of the structure of a promising solution, which is called a priori information, with posterior structure information with good solutions. The main idea is inspired loosely by real ants' behavior, in that the search is conducted in parallel over several computational constructive threads based on local problem data, and the structure of the dynamic memory consists of quality information.

5.3.6 Phases of the Ant Colony Algorithm

The ACO technique is useful to track the intrusion information applied to solve the behavioral analysis of intrusive problems; the involvement of phases used to learn the behavior of intrusive and various iterative manipulations are explained in this section.

5.3.6.1 Phase 1: Initialization Phase

The intrusion can spread randomly around the whole networking system. The following steps are involved in the initialization phase:

- Set pheromone to zero.
- When the intruder starts to work on discovering the target, the pheromone is deposited. PH_S or PH_{SC} indicates a successful attempt.
- If the attempt fails, a pheromone deposit is recorded and is represented as F_PH_S.
- The attempt to visit a network that does not contain a privacy setting is called PH_C.

Complete descriptions about different pheromone parameters to represent the different significant areas by the intruders are given in Table 5.1.

Table 5.1: Pheromone Parameters of Initialization Phase

Pheromone Item		Index	Significance	Notes
Attempt Success	PHs	1	Highly confidential or classified	The intruder successfully visited or entered the area of highest confidentiality.
	PHsc	2	Confidential or classified	The intruder successfully entered or visited the confidential area.
Failure Attempt	F_PHs	3	Highly confidential or classified	The intruder failed to visit the highly confidential area.
	F_PHsc	4	Confidential or classified	The intruder failed to visit the confidential area.
Attempt	PHc	5	General/ not confidential	The intruder visited an area without making a request or having authority

5.3.6.2 Phase 2: Discovery Phase

If the ants (intruders) take an interest in the area (confidential information), the following actions are performed:

- A communication tunnel is constructed and backdoors are established.
- An advanced search, such as browsing websites or searching the database, is performed.
- The trail is hidden and the previous record gets omitted.
- Finally, they leave the place immediately.

5.3.6.3 Phase 3: Re-examination Phase

If food is found by one ant, other ants will follow the same path. Until all the food has been carried out of the area, the pheromone density will increase. The pheromone gradually evaporates once all the food has been carried out. Intruders act in the same way. If a confidential area is found by an intruder, then an organized group of intruders will visit the colony in the network. Different captions and indexes that represent different devices are tabulated in Table 5.2.

Table 5.2: Different Services

Hardware		Software	
I_S	Server	I_{OS}	Operating System
I_R	Router	I_D	Database
I_{SW}	Switch	I_{AP}	Application Program
I_{FW}	Firewall	I_{FD}	File document
I_T	Terminal	I_{SP}	Security Parameter

In the networking system, there are many devices and nodes, so the intruder's movement from the ith node to the jth node can be observed in the stochastic process. The probability model is applied to define and measure the intruders' movement according to equation (I):

$$Ir_{x,y} = \frac{|IH_x - IH_y|^{\sigma}}{\sum_{x,y} |IH_x - IH_y|^{\sigma}}$$

(I)

where:

IH_x denotes the number of pheromones placed on the x node;

IH_y indicates the number of pheromones placed on the y node; and

σ signifies the power parameter used for tuning.

The pheromone density variation on each node IH_DN_i is defined in equation (II):

$$IH\_DN_z = \sum_{z,\rho} IH_z.\beta^{\rho}$$

(II)

where:

z index represents the zth pheromone;

β is the factor of evaporation that lies between the range zero to one; and

ρ is the timing factor.

The time estimated by the timing factor elapses between two consecutive attempts of the ith node.

According to the following equation, the pheromone of each trail can be summarized as:

$$IH\_DN_{i,j} = \sum_{j}\sum_{k,\rho} IH_i . \beta^{\rho}$$

(III)

The different nodes on the trail are represented by j.

The pheromone is updated according to the evaporation factor, the number of attempts and the duration.

5.3.7 Secure Honeypot Architecture

A secure honeypot architecture is developed to avoid worms spreading from the honeypot to other systems in the network. To provide advanced security, the honeypot architecture consists of two main parts:

Data Control Limit: The control of data is limited to prevent the spread of the affected honeypot to the whole network system.

Multi-level IP log table: In system logs, attackers' confidential information is protected in a multi-level IP log table.

5.3.8 Data Control Limit

To prevent the affected honeypot from spreading to the whole network system, a data control limit was used. The data control limit has two processes, which are a connection limit to identify the possibility of connections between attackers and a rate limit.

5.3.9 Multi-level IP log Table (MLIP)

All the activities of intruders cannot be captured by a single layer; all the information is captured by an MLIP about the unwanted intruders' activities like compile, add, file, delete, changes, processes started and keystrokes in system logs. With this method, even if the collected information is destroyed by the hackers in the log server, the information still survives in binary log files.

5.4 SIMULATION RESULTS

5.4.1 Simulation parameters

The Network Simulator (NS-2) is used to simulate the proposed architecture. The simulation's settings and parameters are summarized in Table 5.3.

Table 5.3: Simulation parameters

No. of Nodes	100
Number of Servers	5
Number of Attack Targets	5
Attackers	25, 50 and 75
Simulation Time	10 sec
Interval	1.0
Attack Concentration Level	0,1 and 2
Attacker Rate	0.01Mbps
Packet Size	1000

In Figure 5.6, the simulation topology is shown:

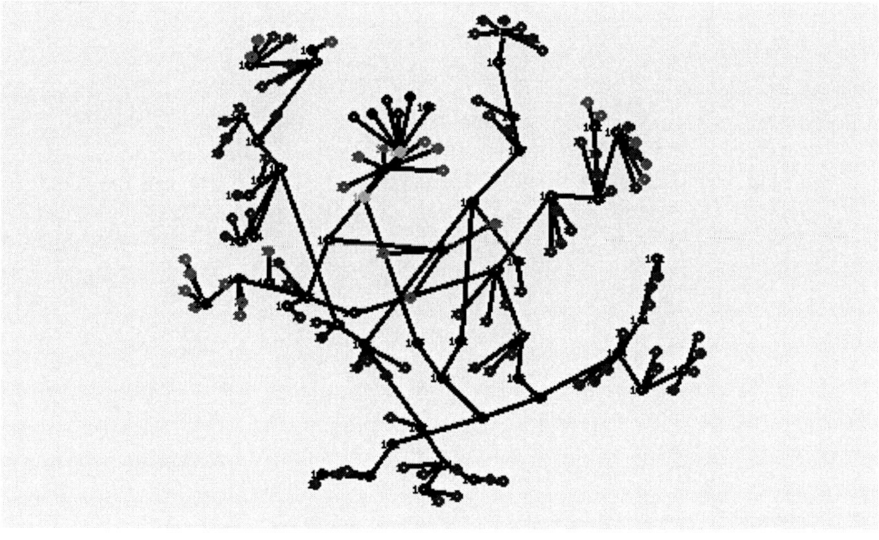

Figure 5.6: Simulation Topology

5.4.2 Performance Metrics and Results

The proposed Ant-based DDoS Detection Technique Using Roaming Virtual Honey Pots (ADTRVH) was compared with the Intelligent Honeypot-Based Detection (IHBD) system (Prathapani *et al.* 2009). The performance was evaluated based on packet delivery ratio, end-to-end delay, throughput and false positives.

5.4.3 Based on Attackers

Here, the attackers launch DDoS flooding attacks towards the victim nodes as well as worm hole attacks directed at the honeypots. The number of attackers was varied between 25, 50 and 75.

Table 5.4: Results of Delay and Delivery Ratio with Respect to Intrusions

No. of intrusions	Delay (Seconds)		Packet Delivery Ratio	
	ADTRVH	IHBD	ADTRVH	IHBD
25	0.442833	0.442833	0.907277	0.907277
50	0.442833	0.448621	0.907277	0.906238
75	0.448621	0.472166	0.936238	0.923491

Figure 5.7 shows the delay that occurred for both the ADTRVH and IHBD techniques. Obviously, the effect of the attackers can increase the end-to-end delay, as depicted in Figure 5.7. But, since the ADTRVH uses the ACO algorithm, the detection time is less than the IHBD. Hence, the delay of the ADTRVH technique is 6% less than for the IHBD.

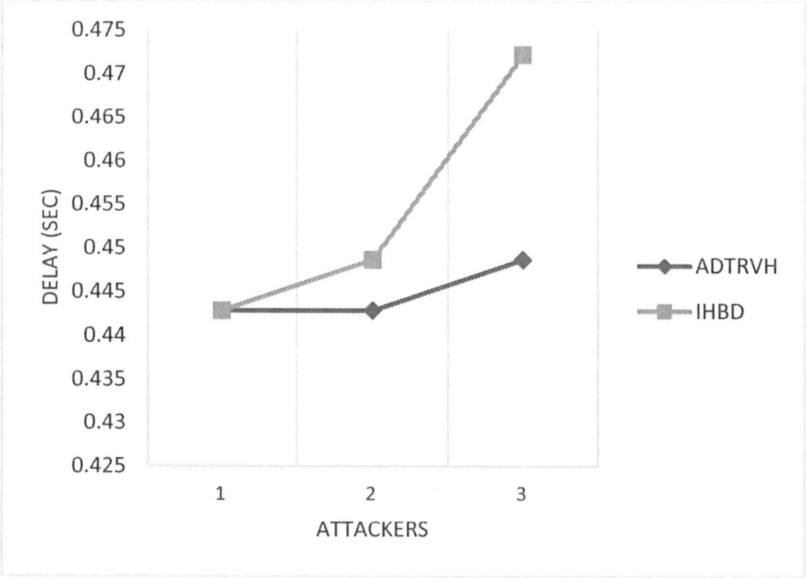

Figure 5.7: Attackers versus Delay

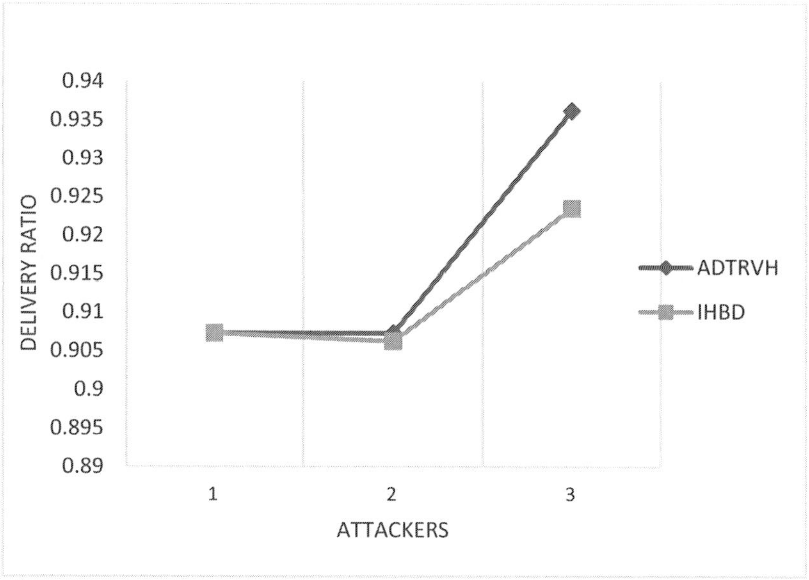

Figure 5.8: Attackers versus Delivery Ratio

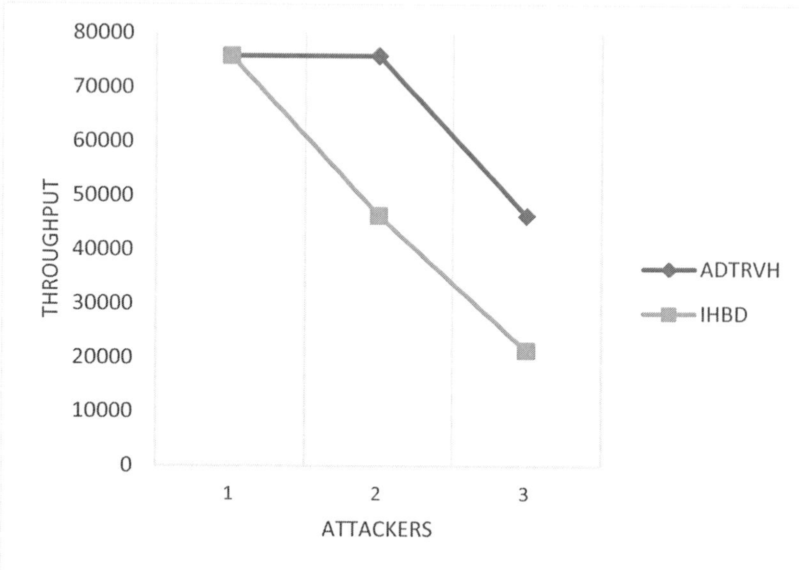

Figure 5.9: Attackers versus Throughput

When the number of attackers is increased from 25 to 100, it results in more packet drops, thereby degrading the delivery ratio and throughput. This behavior can be observed in Figures 5.8 and 5.9, respectively. But the ADTRVH provides additional security for honeypots and ACO-based traceback mechanisms, so the delivery ratio and throughput of the ADTRVH is higher than the IHBD by 3% and 32%, respectively.

Table 5.5: Throughput and false positive values based on intrusion

No. of intrusions	Throughput		False Positives	
	ADTRVH	IHBD	ADTRVH	IHBD
25	75881	75881	15	38
50	75881	46374	20	39
75	46374	21437	25	40

The throughput and false positive values are tabulated in Table 5.5, based on the number of intrusions. Throughput refers to the average successful data or message deliveries over a specific communication link. The ratio is the received number of packets by the destination node to the observation time duration. Throughput determines the overall performance of the system. The throughput is high in the proposed system.

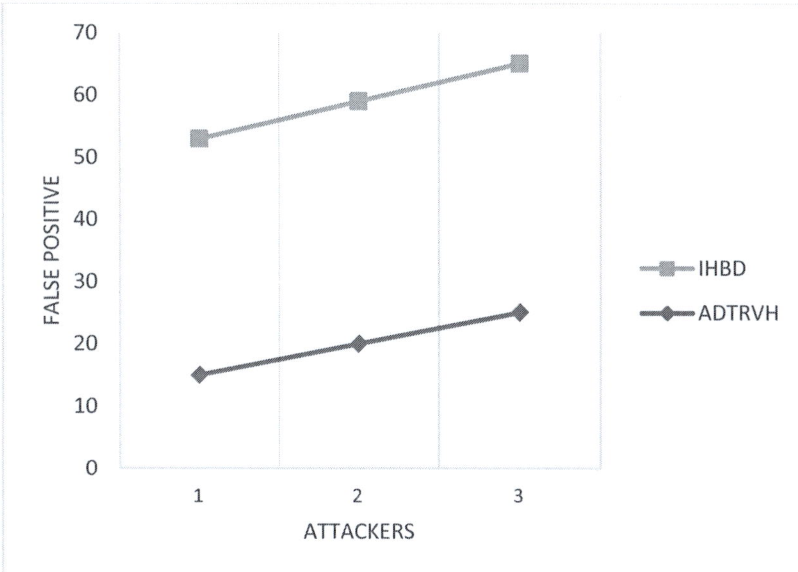

Figure 5.10: Attackers versus False Positives

Figure 5.10 shows the false positives obtained for both techniques when the number of attackers is increased. The false positive percentage increases as the number of attackers is increased. But the ADTRVH performs better when compared to the IHBD by attaining 34% less false positives, as it uses traceback and multi-level log tables.

5.4.4 Based on Attack Concentration Level (ACL)

The ACL specifies the placement of attacker nodes (i.e. sparser or denser). The value 0 corresponds to a low level, 1 corresponds to a medium level and 2 corresponds to a high level. The results are given for these three sets of levels. The number of attackers is kept at 25 for all levels.

Table 5.6: The value of the delay and delivery ratio based on attack concentration level

Attack concentration level	Delay		Delivery ratio	
	ADTRVH	IHBD	ADTRVH	IHBD
0	0.442833	0.472166	0.923491	0.907277
1	0.404575	0.442833	0.907277	0.901544
2	0.376681	0.404575	0.915442	0.911279

The results in the proposed system are for delay, throughput and delivery ratio, based on the attack concentration level. The end-to-end delay slightly increases, as shown in Figure 5.11. The detection time is less because the ADTRVH uses the ACO algorithm, hence the ADTRVH delay is 16% less than for the IHBD.

Additional security is provided by the ADTRVH for honeypots and the mechanism based on the ACO traceback, so the ADTRVH delivery ratio is 4% higher than in the IHBD, as shown in Figure 5.12.

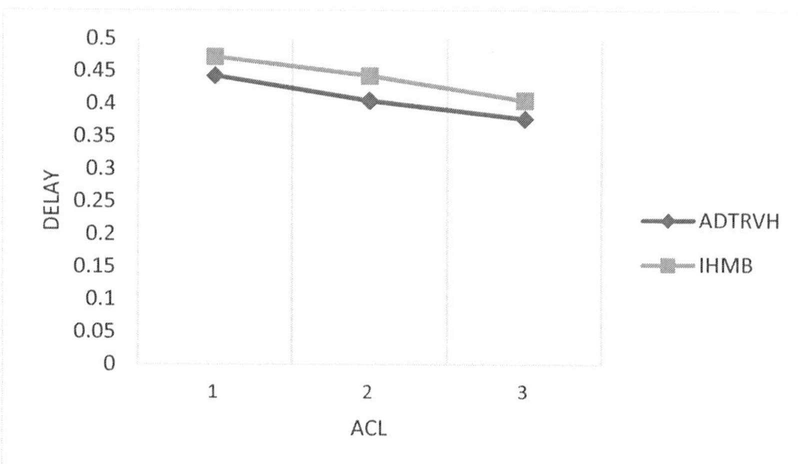

Figure 5.11: ACL versus Delay

Figure 5.11 shows the delay that occurred for the ADTRVH and IHBD techniques. The end-to-end delay increases slightly, as depicted in Figure 5.11. As the ADTRVH uses the ACO algorithm, the detection time is less. Hence, the delay of the ADTRVH is 11% less than the IHBD.

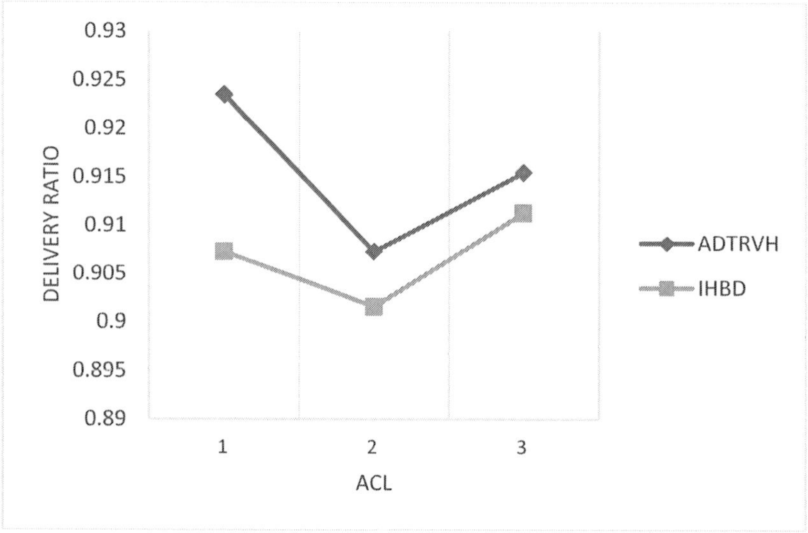

Figure 5.12: ACL versus Delivery Ratio

When the ACL is increased, it results in more packet drops, thereby degrading the delivery ratio. This behavior can be observed in Figure 5.12. But the ADTRVH provides additional security for honeypots and the ACO-based traceback mechanism. The delivery ratio of the ADTRVH is higher than the IHBD by 4%.

Figure 5.13 shows the false positives obtained for both techniques when the ACL is increased. The false positive percentage increases when the ACL is increased. However, the ADTRVH performs better when compared to the IHBD by attaining 20% less false positives, as it uses traceback and multi-level log tables.

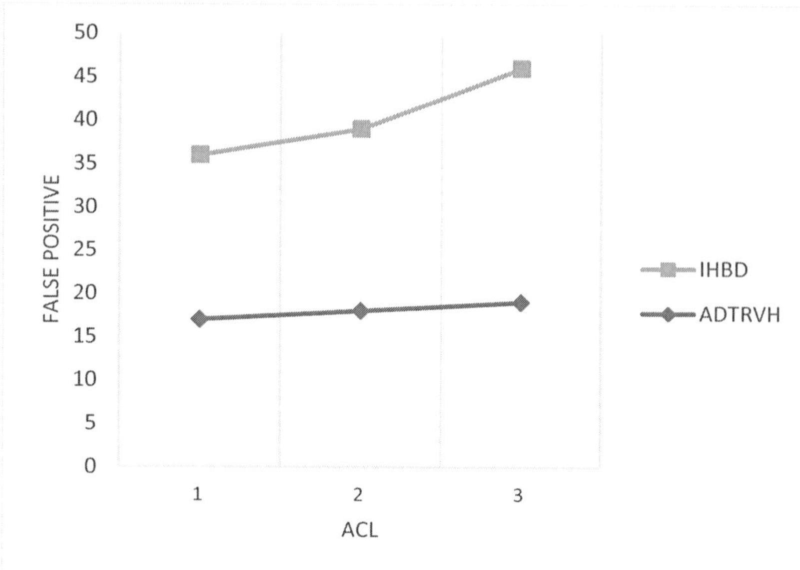

Figure 5.13: ACL versus False Positives

5.5 CONCLUSION

The Ant-based DDoS Detection Technique Using Roaming Virtual Honeypots (ADTRVH) has been proposed in this chapter. Here, together with the secure multi-level architecture (MLA), a virtual roaming honeypot is used to collect information at diverse levels of the network about numerous intruders. Information about the intruders is collected based on the ACO technique, the MLA gets information to limit the intruders' connection with the honeypot, and the spread of intruders even gets stopped. At different levels of the network, the MLIP log table is used to detect intruders. Once the affected area was found, the information was transferred to the MLA to limit the spread of the affected area to the honeypot. Information was sent to the honeypot to build a defense system against the intruder. A simulation of the proposed technique resulted in a reduction in false positives and an increase in the packet delivery ratio and throughput.

CHAPTER 6

ENHANCED INTRUSION DETECTION SYSTEM PERFORMANCE USING A FIRECOL PROTECTION SERVICES-BASED HONEYPOT SYSTEM

6.1 INTRODUCTION

Many security problems have been raised due to the explosion in the usage of networks, the Internet and computers (Moosavi & Bui 2014). CERT reports show that the number of intrusions has increased dramatically. Malicious or intrusion attacks on network vulnerabilities may cause a harmful disaster and destroy security protocols. Security information and network threats are important issues (Idowu *et al.* 2013). To reach statutory compliance and address challenges and threat reduction in security information, tools for information security such as firewalls, antivirus software and intrusion detection systems (Krishnan 2015) have been used in secure multi-level architecture for the discovery of networks or systems under intrusion or attack.

Security is not fully assured by the intrusion detection system, but by using it along with assessments of vulnerability, user authentications, a security policy, access control, and firewalls, IDS and data encryption can greatly improve the security of a network.

There are three important security functions in the intrusion detection system: 1) monitoring, 2) detecting, and 3) responding to illegal activity. To describe certain events, the IDS uses a set of policies; if an issue is detected, an alert or automatic event triggers a response. The response consists of disabling a user account, launching scripts and logging off a user (Sokol *et al.* 2013). In the background of the system, the intrusion detection system runs continuously to monitor the traffic of the network and the computer system and analyze the network traffic (Yu *et al.* 2010). The system administrator relies on tools to monitor and protect the network and system, and he identifies inappropriate activity on a computer or network by checking events, and alerts get forwarded after certain events, like network scanning to resolve computer systems. The activities of inbound and outbound networks are examined by the IDS and doubtful patterns that specify a system or network attack aimed at breaking the system are recognized (Maleh *et al.* 2015).

In misuse detection, data are collected and examined by intrusion detection systems, and the data are compared to huge attack databases or intrusion signatures (Lin *et al.* 2012). In anomaly detection, the choice of anomalies is based on activities in a computer system which do not normally occur. The administrator describes the typical size of a packet, baseline, network traffic load, breakdown and protocol. The data packet flowing through the network is examined, and the malicious data packets are identified by the network intrusion detection system. In host intrusion detection systems (HIDS) or host-based systems, the resource gets power to supervise the HIDS. To identify an intrusion into the host, the HIDS is used. The signature-based intrusion detection (SIDS) works based on attack signatures.

The signatures are stored, or a comparison of events is made against incoming network traffic. An alert is generated if the patterns match at any one time. To learn about the attackers, honeypot systems are introduced to monitor the idle spaces of internet protocol (IP). The benefit of the honeypot system over other existing monitoring solutions is in only gathering suspicious activity. The attacker gets attracted by the honeypot system and is then invited to attack or intrude (Sajana *et al.* 2009). There are five components that are used to handle network intrusion: a load balancer, a token verifier, a mail server, the Firecol protection service and the honeypot.

6.2 PROPOSED WORK

By using the proposed FPSIDS-HPS approach, the intrusion (or attack) can be prevented. The structure of the proposed system is shown in Figure 6.1, which consists of five major components:

1) Initially, the original user is connected to the Internet and then starts the communication process with the Firecol Protection Service, which checks the user status and forwards it to the load balancer.
2) Token keys are generated by the load balancer for the user and for the attacker who is attacking the network. Two different token keys are generated by the load balancer with different ranges. The generated token key is forwarded by the load balancer to the mail server.

3) The key is also sent to the user separately by the mail server, and then it is verified by the token key verifier.
4) The key range is checked with the verifier to identify whether it came from the original user or not. The data are sent to the user by the server after the verification request has been received. If the token key is sent by the attacker, the token range received is different. The request should then be forwarded to the honeypot system.
5) Irrelevant data are transferred by the honeypot to the attacker. A powerful intrusion detection system (IDS) is provided by the honeypot that can be used to determine the intrusion.

6.2.1 Firecol Protection Services

At the level of the ISP (Internet Service Provider), the attacked source and the flooding IDS attacks of the victim host are detected by the Firecol system. Firecol is a distributed architecture built with a large number of ISPs with overlay network connections. These networks are protected with rings for all its customers. The FPS (Firecol Protection Service) has five processes: a) Packet Processor, b) Metrics Manager, c) Selection Manager, d) Score Manager, and e) Collaboration Manager. The traffic, frequencies and counters of every selected rule are recognized by the Packet Processor (PP). During the processing of the packet, a wide variety of algorithms can be applied to the data as the packet moves through the network. Each rule and frequency is computed by the Metrics Manager (MM). A particular instance of rule-based traffic is the traffic filter of the network. The Selection Manager (SM) determines the network traffic profile from the stored ones, etc. The Score Manager (SCM) allocates a core value from the decision table to every rule selected, depending on the frequencies and entropies received from the upstream IPS. The Collaboration Manager (CM) confirms the potential intrusion or attack.

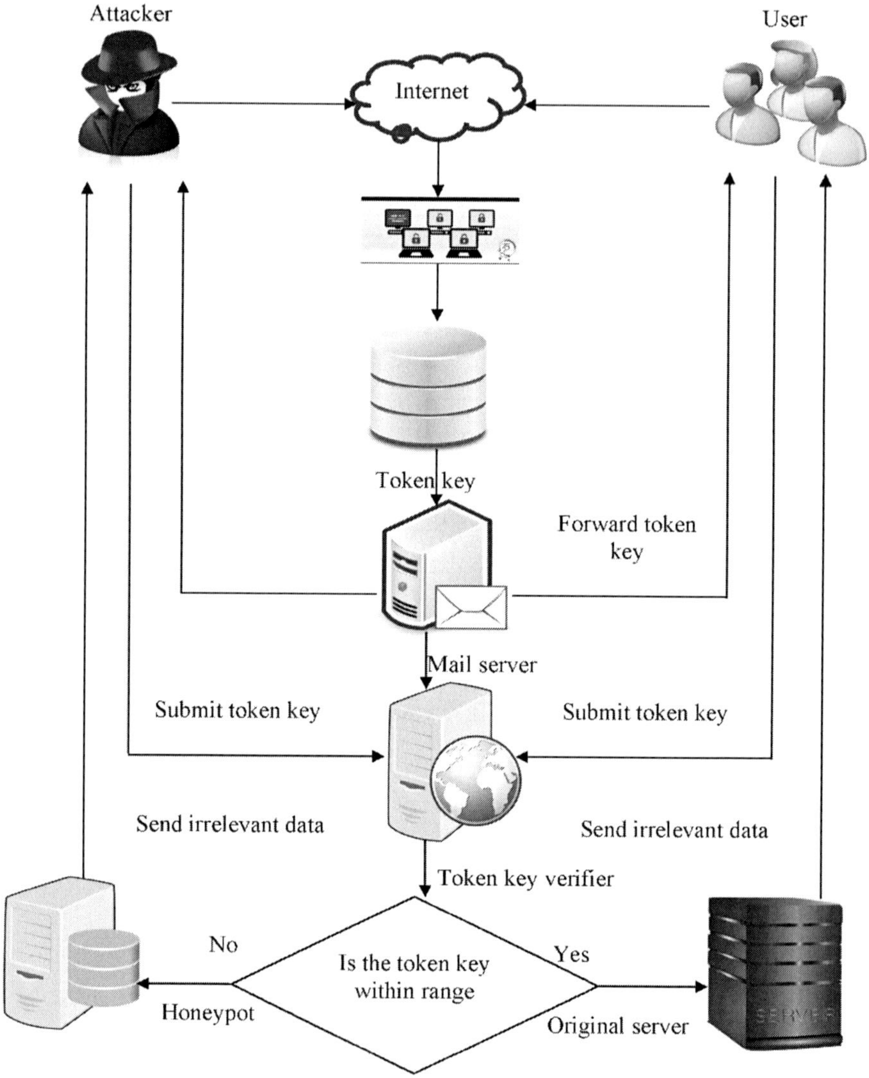

Figure 6.1: Proposed Network Architecture

6.2.2 Load Balancer

In this research, the load balancer generates the tokens for the original user and the attacker. The token is an important part of intrusion detection. The uses of the token are as follows. If the attacker is identified at that time, the IP address and system ID of the attacker are identified by the load balancer. The attacker cannot access the Internet due to the token key. On receiving the Firecol Protection Services result, the decision is taken by the load balancer. If the Firecol Protection Services result indicates the presence of an attack, then the load balancer generates a token for the attack and the token gets forwarded through the mail server to the attacker. Otherwise, the token gets forwarded through the mail server to the original user.

6.2.3 Mail server

"A mail server is the computerized equivalent of the friendly neighborhood mailman" (Aka 2018). There are two main categories in the mail server: outgoing mail servers and incoming mail servers. Outgoing mail servers are known as SMTPs. or Simple Mail Transfer Protocol servers.

The user's details, such as their system ID and IP address, are present in the mail server. The details are forwarded to the mail server after an intruder or attacker connects with the Internet. The server manages the network traffic. The mail server sends the token to the original user and attacker frequently. The token is received by the server from the load balancer, and tokens get forwarded to the user and attacker.

6.2.4 Token verifier

The token verifier is an important component of the proposed system. Once the token is received by the user/attacker, they send the token to the token verifier. The token is received by the token verifier and the structure of the token is checked. If a match occurs between the token structure and the original user, the request is forwarded to the original server. If the structure of the token is matched with the attacker, then the request is forwarded into the honeypot system for irrelevant data transmission.

6.2.5 Honeypot System

The computer security mechanism known as the honeypot is set to deflect, detect (in some manner) and counteract attempts at unauthorized system information usage. This is similar to the police baiting a criminal and then conducting undercover surveillance before the criminal is finally punished.

Honeypots are computer systems developed for logging and monitoring the activities of an entity that intends to attack or compromise the network intrusion (Shih *et al.* 2013). The activities on a honeypot system are considered to be suspicious. Honeypot systems come in many shapes and sizes. For example, the database contains irrelevant items, the traffic component of low interaction networks such as the high interaction of hosts with the operating system, and preconfigured network traffic (Wang *et al.* 2012).

6.3 DEPLOYMENT CLASSIFICATION

Honeypot systems can be categorized by their level of deployment and involvement. Production honeypot systems are simple to use, capture limited information, and are used mainly by companies or corporations; production honeypot systems are positioned within various servers within the production network by the organization to increase overall security. Production honeypot systems are low interaction honeypots, which are deployed in a simple way. A smaller amount of information about the attacks and the attackers is provided compared to research honeypots. The production honeypot system intends to mitigate risk support in an organization. The value of the security measures of the organization is included in the honeypot. Research honeypot systems are run by non-profit research organizations. The data about the tactics and motives of the black-hat group in targeting various networks are collected by an educational institution or a volunteer.

This honeypot system does not include direct values; the honeypot is used for systematic investigation, and the threats an organization is facing are studied to provide better protection against them. The information is used for protection against threats. The honeypot system is difficult to deploy and maintain, and is used mainly by government, research, and military organizations for far-reaching information capture. Vulnerable resources, like open mail relays and open proxies, are misused by spammers. The honeypot source code is created by system administrators (SAs), who impersonate these vulnerable resources to find out the activities of spammers.

In a honeypot system, there are various capabilities it can provide SAs with, and such irrelevant systems make misuse more complex and risky. The powerful action of the honeypot system can be taken to misuse that maximum value of misuse (e.g. spammers). The honeypot system can reveal the misused IP address that provides the bulk spam capture.

It is possible to find out the e-mail addresses spammers use in open relay honeypots as the destination for test messages. To discover open relays, spammers are used. To mislead the spammer, some unlawful relay electronic mail gets sent to the dropbox email address. The real misusable open relay is the honeypot system, and the honeypot system frequently gets to respond by sending a huge amount of relay spam to the honeypot and stops it. The source may be a different misused system chain that spammers and attackers use to make the original starting point of the misused traffic difficult to detect.

6.3.1 E-mail trap

An e-mail address used for getting spam can be identified as spam. By comparing the honeypot with the spam trap, we can see it should be reserved for systems and methods used to counter attacks and detect problems. Spam reaches the destination in the same way that the arrival of non-spam e-mail takes place. The open source project utilizes honeypot pages on its website in some regions of the world. The honeypot pages exclusively hand out e-mail addresses that are tagged as spam. By harvesting e-mail addresses, spammers can use the honeypot system's pathway to collect and send spam to an e-mail address.

6.3.2 Honeypot Database

Intruders frequently attack databases with the use of Structured Query Language (SQL). The firewall of the fundamental network does not identify certain activities. Network firewall databases are frequently used by organizations.

6.4 RESULTS AND DISCUSSION

6.4.1 Experimentation

For the measurement of the proposed approach's performance, a sequence of experiments was conducted on the extracted dataset. Two thousand connection records are included in the extracted dataset with a set of forty features based on the connection and a label that clearly defines the connection status. The features are split into four groups: (i) common features of Transmission Control Protocol (TCP) connections, including the duration of the connection and the network service; (ii) domain knowledge, which suggests the features of the content inside a connection for the payload evaluation of the TCP of original packets like the amount of failed login attempts; (iii) the recognized connection, which is observed by the host feature in the past two seconds and which has a similar target to the current connection of a host and computes the statistics related to the service and behavior of protocol, etc.; and (iv) service features, which examine the connections made in the past two seconds that have an equivalent service to the present connection.

Table 6.1: Attribute fragmentation from the IP address

S. No.	Attribute
1	Duration
2	Protocol type
3	Service
4	Flag
5	Source bytes
6	Destination bytes
7	Number of failed logins
8	Service received error rate
9	Different service rate
10	Destination host count

The partial attribute names obtained from network datasets are shown in Table 6.1. The fragmented details about the normal dataset are shown in Table 6.2. The datasets were collected from the policies of internet service providers of various communication networks because internet service providers' policies can differ from one another.

Table 6.2: Normal big dataset fragmentation

ID	Duration	Flag	Source byte	Destination byte
1	81	18	522	0
2	12	61	0	0
3	22	61	0	0
4	65	184	520	0
5	45	47	0	0
6	66	28	522	0
7	78	132	18	0
8	45	134	0	0
9	74	58	89	0
10	35	1	50	0

Table 6.3: Number of logins versus number of malicious users

No. of logins	Detected malicious user ratio
1000	40
2000	50
3000	58
4000	42
5000	69
6000	51
7000	73
8000	80
9000	82
10000	70

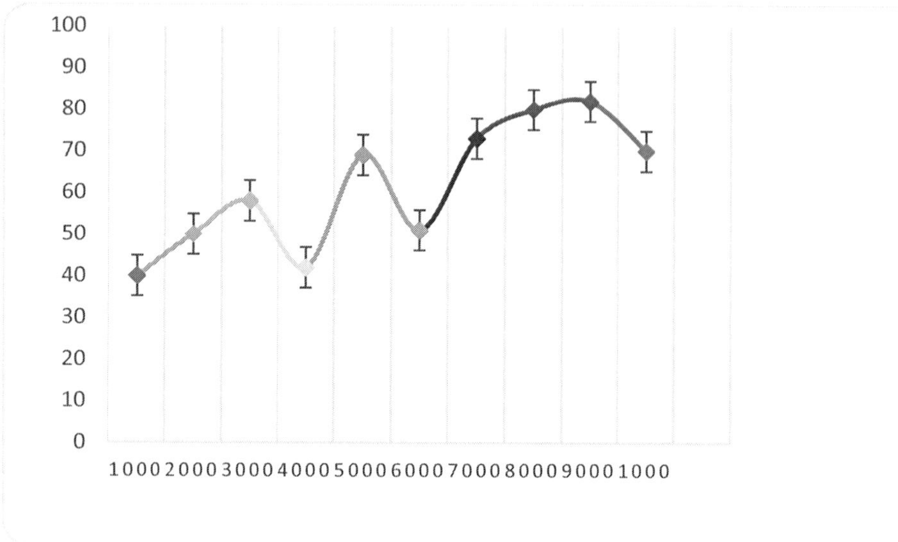

Figure 6.2: Number of logins versus number of malicious users

Table 6.4: Number of malicious requests and honeypot responses based on time interval

Time interval	No. of malicious requests	No. of honeypot responses
1	8000	3000
2	10000	4500
3	12000	7000
4	12000	7000
5	14000	8000
6	17000	7500
7	19000	9000
8	13000	7500
9	9000	6000
10	15000	8000

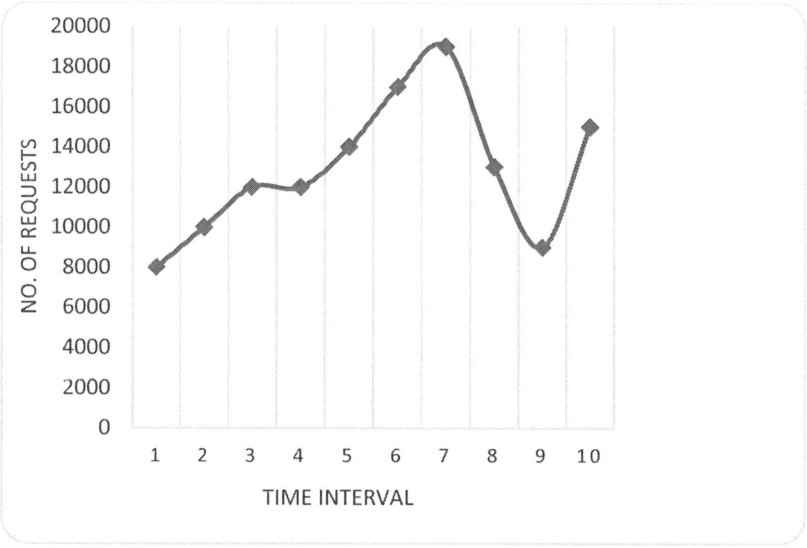

Figure 6.3: Time interval versus number of requests

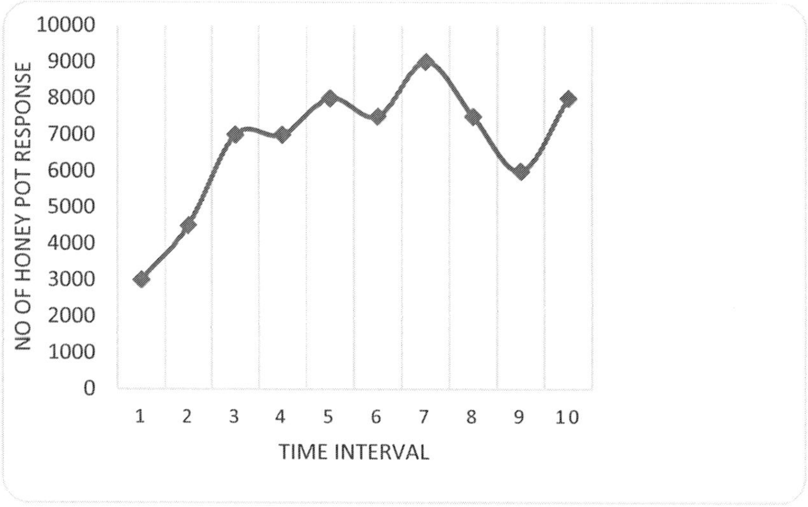

Figure 6.4: Time interval versus number of honeypot responses

The number of malicious requests based on the time interval and the honeypot's responses is tabulated in Table 6.4, and the respective graphical representations are given in Figures 6.3 and 6.4. The CPU utilization process is explained in Table 6.5.

Table 6.5: Number of tokens versus computation overhead of the proposed system

No. of tokens	Computation overhead
2500	35
5000	42
7500	42
10000	40
12500	49
15000	40
17500	53
20000	65
22500	60
25000	55
27500	60
30000	70
32500	60
35000	62

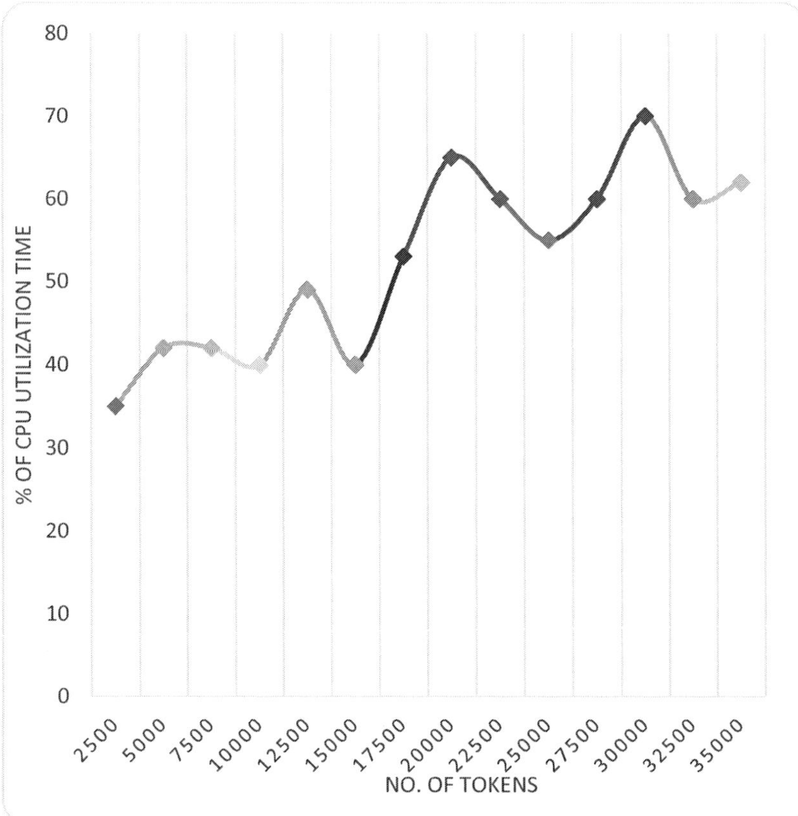

Figure 6.5: Number of tokens versus percentage of CPU utilization time

Table 6.6: Delay and packet delivery ratio values based on number of nodes

No. of nodes	Delay		Packet delivery ratio	
	Proposed	**Existing**	**Proposed**	**Existing**
20	9.247574	15.07536	1.998332	1.184182
40	6.372673	6.099619	1.997468	1.05548
60	10.15263	16.40505	1.995149	1.107477
80	9.103199	9.858383	1.994325	1.089215
100	10.90003	12.25311	1.991925	1.069159

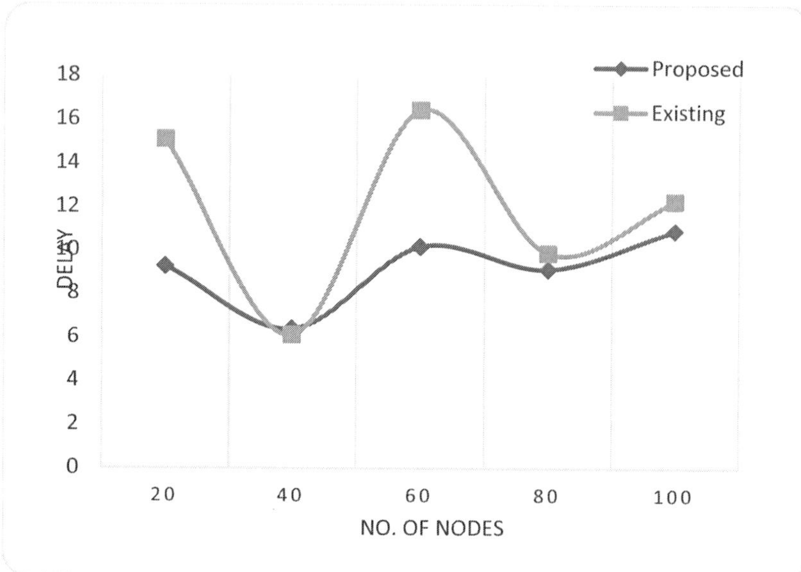

Figure 6.6: Number of nodes versus delay

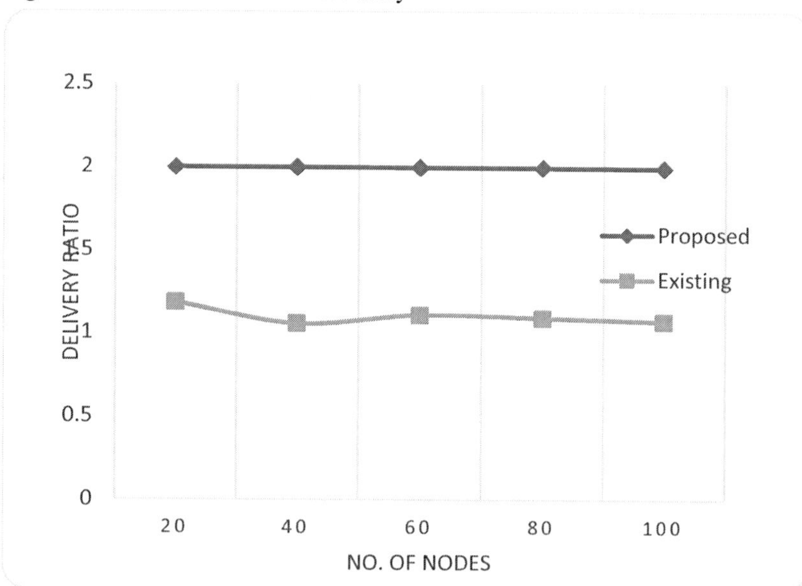

Figure 6.7: Number of nodes versus packet delivery ratio

The delay and packet delivery ratio based on the number of nodes is tabulated in Table 6.6. The delay of the proposed and existing methods is calculated when transferring the data from one node to another. Figure 6.6 shows the number of nodes versus delay. The delay in the proposed method is less compared to the existing method. The packet delivery ratio is the ratio of actual packets delivered to the total packets sent. The number of nodes versus packet delivery ratio is shown in Figure 6.7. The packet delivery ratio is higher compared to the existing method.

Table 6.7: Packet drop and residual energy values based on number of nodes

No. of nodes	Packet drop		Residual energy	
	Proposed	Existing	Proposed	Existing
20	58	1432	24947	5.672106
40	73	4456	25035	6.102247
60	75	7656	24385	6.733925
80	122	8301	24129	6.464328
100	141	10276	23848	6.128423

The packet drop and residual energy values based on the number of nodes are tabulated in Table 6.7. Packet drop denotes the packets discarded in the network at a given moment when a router or other network device is overloaded and cannot accept additional packets. The packet drop in the proposed method is much less compared to the existing method, as shown in Figure 6.8. Figure 6.9 shows the number of nodes versus residual energy. The residual energy for each node in the proposed method is high.

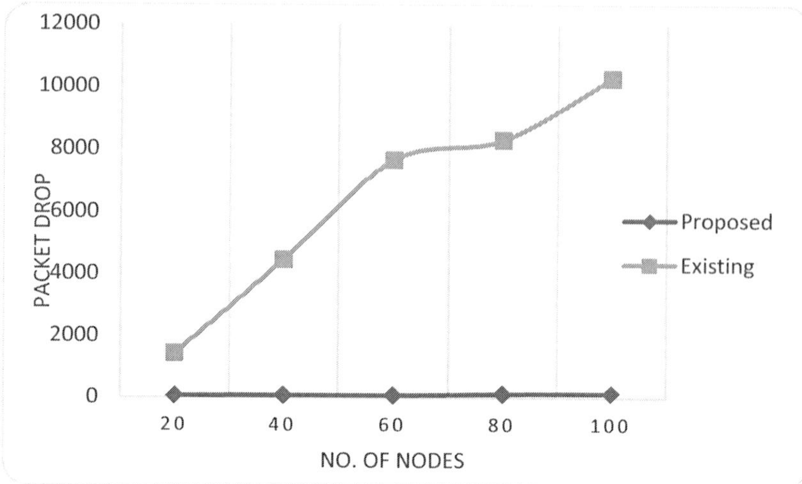

Figure 6.8: Number of nodes versus packet drop

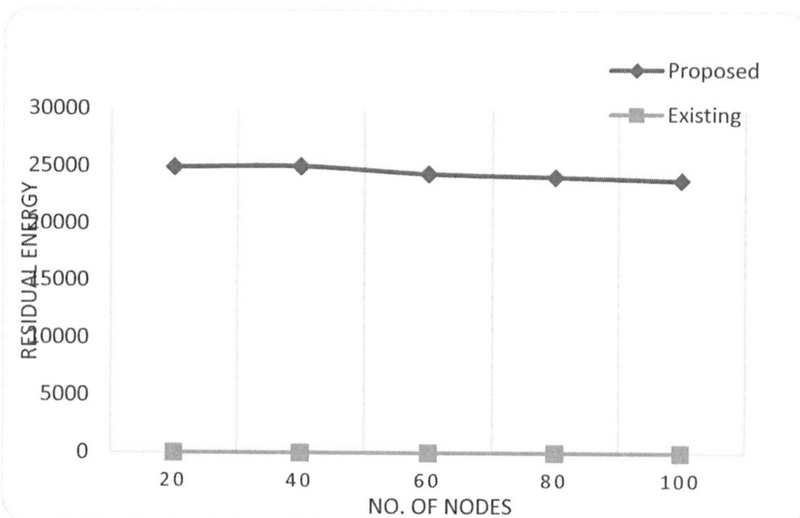

Figure 6.9: Number of nodes versus residual energy

Table 6.8: Overhead and throughput values based on number of nodes

No. of nodes	Overhead		Throughput	
	Proposed	Existing	Proposed	Existing
20	12703	19700	12703	19700
40	13023	27987	14023	26987
60	13343	26478	15343	24478
80	13663	27856	15663	22856
100	14983	27857	15983	26857

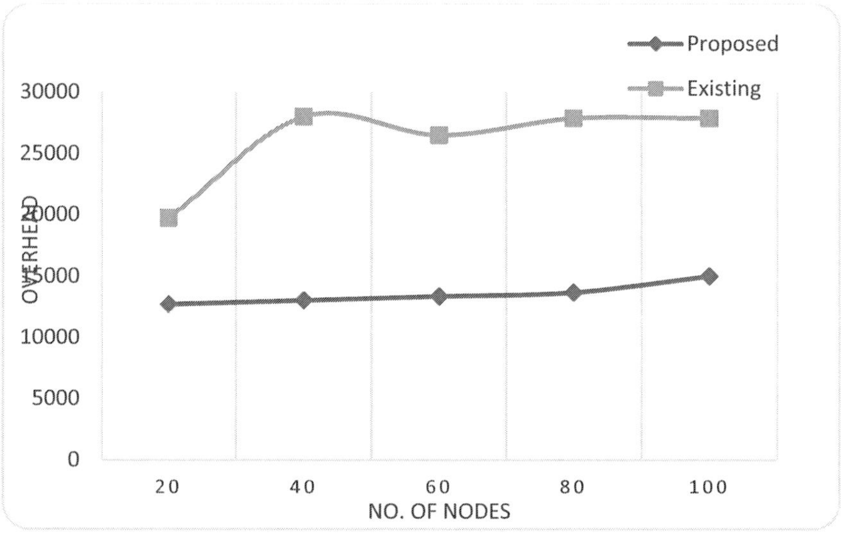

Figure 6.10: Number of nodes versus overhead

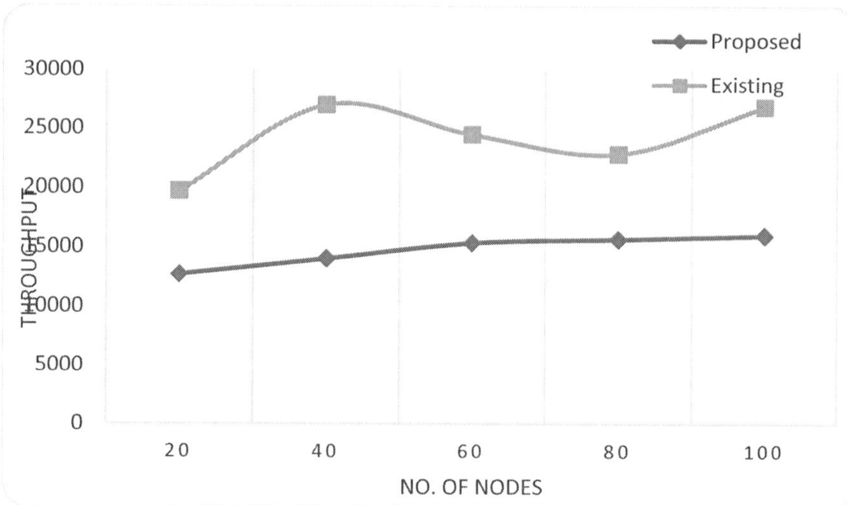

Figure 6.11: Number of nodes versus throughput

The number of nodes versus overhead is shown in Figure 6.10, and Figure 6.11 shows the number of nodes versus throughput. The overhead of the proposed system is less compared to the existing method and the throughput is high, which makes the system performance high.

6.5 CONCLUSION

A Firecol Protection Service-based Honeypot System (FPS-HPS) was proposed in order to reduce network intrusion in a computer network. A load balancer, the Firecol Protection Service, and the honeypot system are present in the proposed approach, which improves the performance of the intrusion detection system. The load balancer generates tokens for the authenticated user and the attacker, based on the result of the Firecol Protection Service. In the load balancer and the Firecol system, unnecessary computation and communication are avoided. Time and cost are reduced for malicious internet packets. The proposed honeypot system is an irrelevant information handling system. The research purpose of the honeypot description is to show its value to the security system community. The proposed honeypot system can be used for the purpose of production by detecting, preventing and responding to attacks. The research usage of the proposed honeypot system includes the collection of information about threats in order to understand and defend against them more efficiently.

CHAPTER 7

EIDPS: AN EFFECTIVE TECHNIQUE TO SECURE THE NETWORK FROM INTRUSION

7.1 INTRODUCTION

Security maintenance is one of the major significant roles that is played out in IT. In the course of the most recent decade, the IT environment has accomplished major advancements due to the fact that nobody wants their framework to be intruded and thus allow their data to be interrupted by an attacker (Wang *et al.* 2012). General web usage in day to day life is expanding and thus creating security against interruptions as well as intruders present in the systems, thereby giving dependable services and accessibility to clients, is turning out to be extremely fundamental. Different systems, for example DMZ (Demilitarized Zone) firewalls, have been utilized but they are not very viable (Shih *et al.* 2013). The intrusion detection system (IDS) has been put forward as the best form of system protection when compared to other different procedures. The IDS continually runs in the background of a framework, it watches traffic on the PC as well as the network frameworks, and then it investigates network traffic for potential system interruptions starting from outside the firm as well as framework assaults or misuse from inside the firm.

The system administrator relies on a few devices to protect and screen their networks and system. The administrator identifies the relevant as well as irrelevant actions or utilization of a PC framework or system by analyzing its activities and sending alarms when specific functions happen, like examining system traffic to resolve linked computer systems. An ID is a programming device or mechanism that watches a network or system for malicious functions and submits information to the administrator. A few procedures have tried to stop unauthorized access: the IDPS (Intrusion Detection Prevention System) is basically focused on distinguishing possible occurrences, making log records and sending information back that relates to the attackers (Wang *et al.* 2013).

Moreover, organizations utilize the IDPS for different functions, such as recognizing issues with system security strategies, traditional threats, and recording and keeping individual users from breaking the security policies. The IDPS has turned into an essential for secure communication in every firm. The honeypot system technology is a powerful supplement for the IDS, and has the capacity to decrease its burden (Abduvaliyev *et al.* 2013). The traditional IDS has been proposed according to honeypot technology, and an IDS should be checked back by means of the mobile client to achieve interoperability between its constituent parts; consequently, the honeypot technique is utilized to get the most encouraging results for further attack tracking as well as data signatures to attain automatic data (Butun *et al.* 2014).

IDSs are ordered into two types: the anomaly detection system and the misuse detection system. These classifications are based on different intrusion detection strategies. Misuse detection systems (MDSs) can recognize past classified patterns of known assaults, but unknown assaults' designs cannot be inferred. Anomaly detection systems (ADSs) instead utilize most frameworks with current procedures as well as past procedures in order to evaluate new techniques and to detect unknown assaults viably. The attack method is more troublesome, as unique pattern matching or statistical analysis strategies make it hard to find the number of system assaults (attacks). More traditional IDSs have no ability to trace the information; it is difficult to identify the attack source as well as the intrusion that is being made by the attacker.

Traditional IDSs and other security products cannot function in an interoperable manner. Consequently, our proposed framework executes a new application termed the Enhanced Intrusion Detection Prevention System (EIDPS) to overcome the above-mentioned problems. Our proposed approach includes a combination of techniques, for example, Snort IDS, Sebek, Dionaea, IDS, a honeypot framework and a characterization application similar to the SVM (Support Vector Machine). It likewise utilizes a server-client framework design that is made up of a single primary server and a few clients.

The user provides data about the most significant records together with the malicious codes. At that point, the data is forwarded to the main server for further processing. The server, in turn, analyzes the gathered data packets and, after this process, considers whether it is a fundamental security warning or not. We utilize the IDPS together with the SVM to analyze packets and attacks. If the data is considered as an assault, it sends the data towards the honeypot framework and transmits false information.

7.2 MOTIVATION

The aim of the proposed work is to avoid intrusion occurrences in the network. Thus, the Enhanced Interruption Detection Prevention system is proposed. Our framework gives real-time security to approved clients with the support of Snort, Sebek and Dionaea. The classification of attackers is done by utilizing the intrusion detection prevention system. With the help of the proposed approach, efficient security is achieved throughout the entire network by avoiding unknown third-party attackers.

7.3 INTERRUPTION DETECTION SYSTEMS

An intrusion detection system (IDS) is an instrument that identifies irregular or suspicious activity and focuses on addressing the issues as fast as could reasonably be expected. Given their functional value, IDSs have been focused on more in recent years, keeping in mind that the end goal is to enhance their viability. The products of these studies are various classes of IDSs that depend on various detection approaches, each of which is more suitable for a specific approach. Among others, we discover the intrusion detection systems called HIDS that construct their choices with respect to the data found in machines, and intrusion detection systems called NIDS that construct their choices exclusively in terms of data streaming in a system. More explanations on the different classes of IDSs and their development can be found in Han *et al.* (2013).

7.3.1 Vulnerability of Systems

An assault is an attack on the weaknesses in a network. In this way, decreasing the number of assaults requires a fair knowledge of the network and conceivable approaches to weaknesses so as to discover reasonable protections. The word 'vulnerability' communicates every one of the shortcomings of a computer's assets that can be exploited by malicious users. The appearance of vulnerabilities in data frameworks are due to the following reasons, among others: good security is typically extremely expensive and most companies do not have adequate finances to bear the costs of this need; the security applications that are utilized cannot be 100% certain and are frequently ineffectual; and security strategies are normally complex, inadequate and can be time-consuming.

7.3.2 Categories of Security Attacks

We realize that the primary ability of computer networks is to give data as well as resources to users. In this manner, there is a stream of information that is traded between a source and a destination on a channel. The assignment of the security framework is to restrict access to information and resources so that only the licensed parties (individuals or systems) are permitted to utilize them, as per the security methods introduced. The ordinary stream of information or data is focused on a few classes of security assaults, as shown by Chen *et al.* (2013).

Intrusion: The framework is eliminated or becomes inaccessible. This is an assault on accessibility.

Interception: An unapproved party has gained information by listening to the channel. This is an assault on secrecy.

Change: The information is blocked and altered by an unapproved third party. This is an assault on honesty.

Masquerade: The assailant pretends to be a legitimate source, and accesses the information you need. This is an assault on authentication.

7.3.3 Differences between IDS and IPS

Recently, IDSs have been used to administrate congestion in genuine traffic to increase detection accuracy and diminish false positive rates. On a few occasions, an IPS takes methods from intrusion detection.

The IPS can be utilized as an alarm for attacks inside a system and accommodate attack prevention with firewall and IDS operation applications. In Figure 7.1, we have outlined an examination of an IPS and IDS. An IPS, like an IDS, is implemented to distinguish and identify potential security anomalies in the information stream.

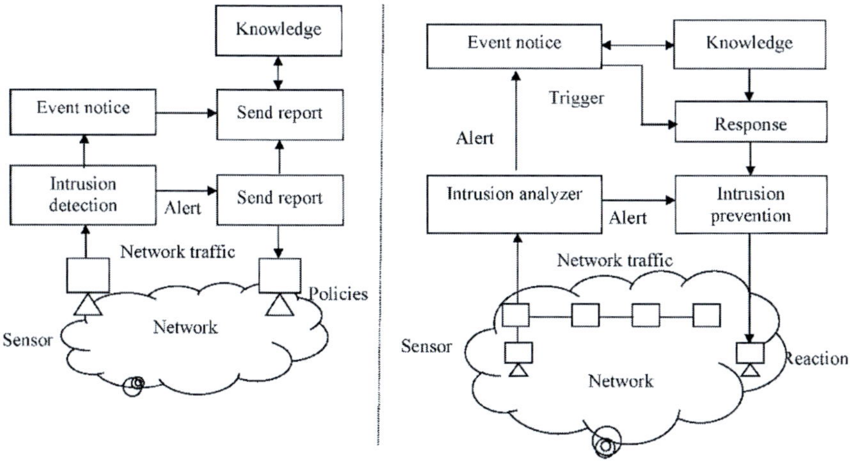

Figure 7.1: Comparison between an IDS (left) and an IPS (right)

However, essential (primary) intrusion detection utilizes the signature application to recognize system traffic and aims to accomplish inbound detection – outbound packets would be sent to corrupt that action before the threat gains access to network assets. IPS joins the strategy firewall with that of the IDS, appropriately using the hands-on method. Another example of a framework to protect organized frameworks and keep attackers away from accessing the system by analyzing different information records and avoiding malicious nodes is the acknowledgment sensor. When an assault is recognized, the intrusion detection system blocks and logs the provided information. The primary commitment is the improvement of a learning stage, which means mapping the issue and demonstrating the test of the IPS.

7.3.4 Detection Analysis:

It is hard to identify one issue that is met with complete recognition in IPS and which examines packet traffic movement.

There are two classes of identification techniques, as shown in Figure 7.2.

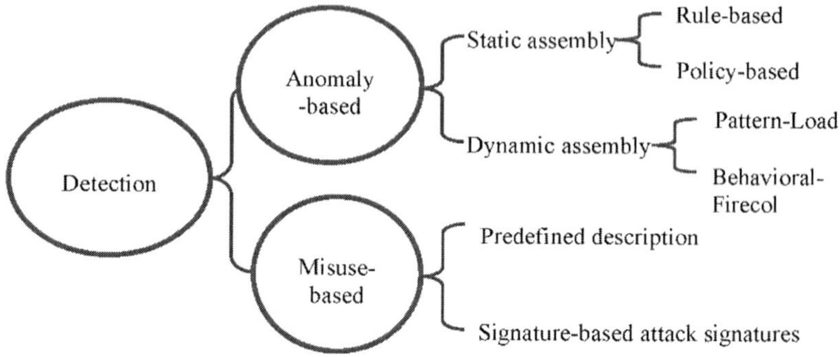

Figure 7.2: Anomaly-based and misuse-based detection systems

1) Anomaly-based: Anomaly-based identification is the method of utilizing anomaly recognition techniques in the identified area, which works in a straightforward way yet with a basic theory. Anomaly identification has the ability to distinguish new sorts of intrusions and requires profile information listed as ordinary information, manufactures a model of typical behavior and naturally identifies any disturbance to it to produce an alert. As indicated by some past work (Tian & Gao 2009), there are two procedures used to estimate anomaly detection:

(i) Threshold identification
(ii) Statistical measures

Anomaly detection looks for intrusion attacks by measuring network traffic with those set up to satisfy the typically used designs gained from prepared information (Subba *et al.* 2016). These are divided into three classifications of anomaly identification strategies based on the way they are handled: (i) measurement-based, (ii) information-based and (iii) machine learning-based. The advantage of this approach is that it has the ability to distinguish new attacks for which signatures have not yet been characterized. However, this approach produces numerous false positive alerts and it is very time consuming for research applications to acquire accurate measurements and extensive profiles of typical conduct. This implies that it requires lengthy arrangements for preparing the information that comprises the environment framework log.

2) Misuse-based: Analysis from misuse locations distinguishes intrusions by coordinating inferred information with a pre-characterized explanation of interfering behavior. In addition, in this approach, a danger is identified by inspecting the network traffic looking for direct matches with a known model of packets (mark or guidelines). Furthermore, it clearly delineates the distinction between misuse-based and anomaly-based identification, which relates to snort rule structure.

Accordingly, a limitation of this approach is that it can only recognize intrusions that match a pre-characterized rule, and the arrangement of the signature always needs to be physically updated to know the new danger. Luckily, this technique can be exceptionally accurate for providing increasingly precise alerts to learn about attacks and their varieties. Moreover, the misuse-based approach generates a low false positive rate.

7.4 IDPS (INTRUSION DETECTION AND PREVENTION SYSTEM) COMPONENTS

The components of the most feasible sections of IDPSs are:

- **Sensor/Agent:** The word ‘sensor’ is utilized for IDPSs that monitor systems, including system-based, remote (wireless), and system behavior examination approaches. The word ‘agent’ is utilized for host-based IDPS technologies.
- **Database Server:** Used as a repository for event data recorded by the sensors or agents handled by the management server.
- **Management Server:** Centralized devices that receive, break down and oversee event data from the sensor/agent. It recognizes events that the sensor/agent cannot.
- **Console**: Provides an interface for the users as well as for the administrator. Console programming is regularly installed onto standard PCs, giving both administrative and checking abilities.

IDPSs are separated by the sorts of occasions that they can perceive and the strategies that they use to recognize incidents on the network.

7.4.1 Types of IDPSs

IDPSs log a broad range of information that is identified with particular events in the system (Wang *et al.* 2008).

- **Host-Based:** Monitors the characteristics of a single host and the events occurring inside that host for suspicious activity. Examples of the types of activities a host-based IDPS may screen are system activity, system logs, running processes, application actions, file access and verification, and network configuration changes. The host-based approach is directed towards basic accessed servers, for example, freely accessible servers (Ahmed & Rajeswari 2012).

- **Network-Based:** Detects network traffic for special network fragments or devices and examines the system and application protocol action to recognize the suspicious action. It can distinguish a wide range of types of attacks. It is generally implemented at a boundary between networks, virtual private network servers, remote access servers, and remote systems.
- **Hybrid:** The utilization of both host-based and network-based IDPSs at the same time.
- **Network Behavior Analysis (NBA):** Examines network traffic in order to identify dangers that produce irregularly congested flows, for example, Denial of Service (DoS) assaults, certain types of malware, and policy violations. NBA frameworks are frequently deployed to monitor internal network flows and are at times used to monitor flows between an association's internal networks and external networks (Shen *et al.* 2011).

7.4.2 IPS Characteristics

An IPS is characterized by two systems that continuously attempt to recognize as well as interrupt malicious system movements. By and large, there are two classifications:

- Rate-based systems
- Content-based systems (also known as signature-based and anomaly-based systems)

The system is frequently used with a firewall and regularly uses a few basic firewall approaches. In any case, firewalls obstruct all movement, with the exception of that which they are authorized to allow, while the IPS transfers all activity aside from that which they are authorized to direct to intrusion detection and prevention systems.

➢ **Rate-based IPS (Intrusion Prevention System)**

Rate-based intrusion prevention techniques congest traffic by taking into account the load of the network, for instance, an excessive amount of packets, an excessive number of interfaces, or an excessive number of faults. When more approaches are seen, the rate-based intrusion prevention system meets with as well as causes congestion, and generally interferes with the activity. Highly valuable rate-based IPSs incorporate groups of configuration alternatives along with responsive technologies.

The rate-based intrusion prevention system additionally holds the maximum traffic occurrence threshold measure over the service. If it goes beyond the threshold limit, the entire function is overloaded.

➢ **Content-based IDS**

Content-based intrusion detection systems congest the relation between attack signatures and protocol faults; they are a crucial development over firewalls and intrusion detection systems. Packets that do not consent to TCP/IP RFCs ought to be eliminated. For example, each port examines and initiates malicious conduct into the IPS to congest further oncoming movement that originated from the host that is unique.

The most appropriate IPS-based function promotes a range of techniques in order to identify the fake information as well as offers numerous choices for the management of attacks, for example, basically dropping malicious packets. The content-based IPS promotes security strategy authorization and it may regularly require diminished support, adjusting itself to perform at a more efficient level than the rate-based IPS.

7.5 OVERVIEW

7.5.1 Proposed System Components

Our Enhanced Intrusion Detection Prevention System (EIDPS) includes two distinct parts: the client and the server.

7.5.2 Client

In order to gather data about the behavior of an intruder or attacker, clients are positioned in a similar context. The client segments self-administer one another and can be activated independently.

The data that has been gained is returned to the main server in order to carry out further system analysis as well as security updates. The client segment contributes three vital devices: the Dionaea client, Snort IDS and the Sebek Client.

A. Snort IDS

SIDS centers transmitted data packets at the time of the intrusion detection process. It likewise identifies the different attack patterns, warning messages and information.

B. Dionaea Client

This client attracts intruders and keeps malware away by simulating vulnerabilities as well as essential services.

C. Sebek Client

The Sebek client records the malicious activity that is performed by the intruder or assailant during the course of the period of communication with the honeypot system in logs.

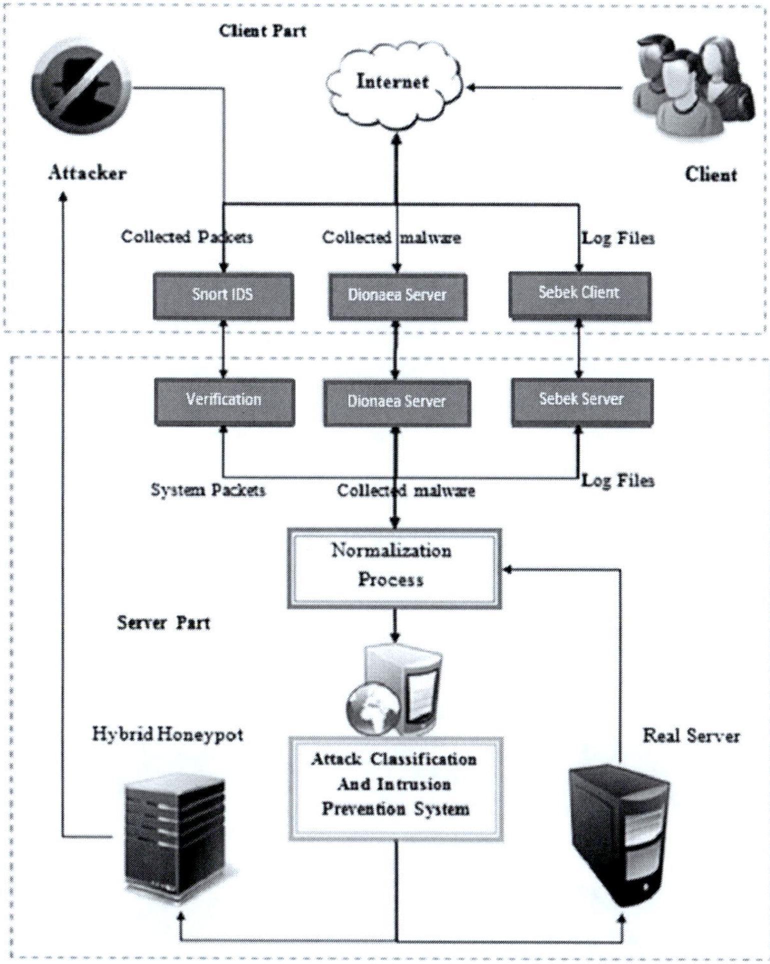

Figure 7.3: System architecture

7.5.3 Server

The main server ought to be connected to a few clients, and it also ought to be centralized. All the received logs are put away onto a database. The server portion is comprised of six critical parts: verifier, Dionaea server, Sebek server, attack classification system, honeypot framework and SVM.

A. Verifier

The verifier is utilized for the verification of packets that have been gained by the Snort IDS. Furthermore, it may likewise check all the client's packets.

B. Dionaea server

The Dionaea server permits malicious codes to be transmitted over to the Dionaea client component.

C. Sebek server

The Sebek server acquires as well as separates various functions that denote the directions to or links with the received data storing process.

D. Intrusion Prevention System

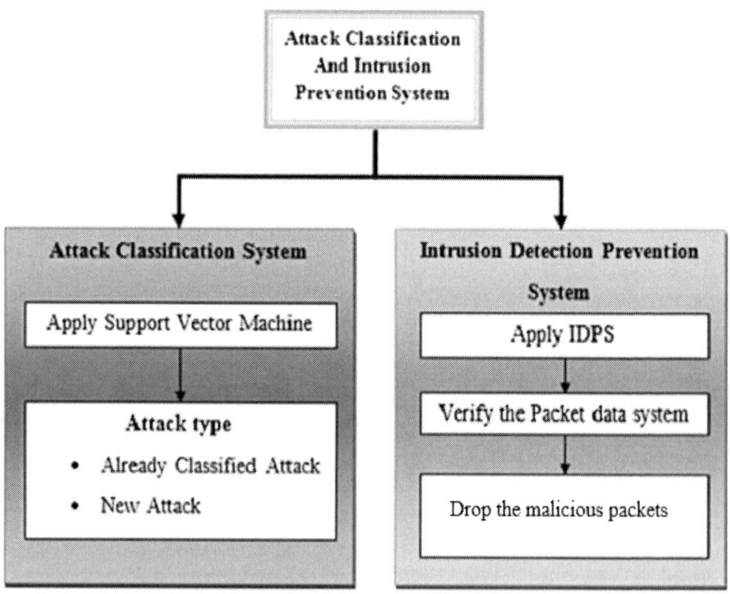

Figure 7.4: Attack classification, IDPS design

Figure 7.4 depicts the design based on attack classification as well as an intrusion prevention system.

One of the most common security mechanisms is the IDPS, which may monitor network and system functions for unauthorized access. IDPSs are made up of two major types: HIDPS and NIDPS. The major functions of an IDPS are the identification of malicious activity and making a move to stop/block it. It is able to perform two operations: detection and prevention. At first, the IPS watches for suspicious activity as well as network traffic, after which it reacts to the malicious network activity by ceasing the access of the client or otherwise blocking the IP address of the network. The IPS acts according to the assumption that the attacker's conduct is different from a legitimate client.

There are three sorts of IDS: anomaly detection, misuse detection, and hybrid detection systems. An IDS ought to perform a few activities like obstructing network traffic, dropping malicious information packets, sending an alert and blocking the connection that originated from the malignant Internet Protocol address. An IPS has the capacity to rectify the malignant information packet flow, CRC errors, eliminate TCP (Transmission Control Protocol) problems, clean up an inefficient system and transport layer options.

E. SVM

The SVM performs regression and classification tasks by generating non-linear decision boundaries. The issue is finding these boundaries; this classification algorithm demonstrates a high level of adaptability in taking care of regression tasks and the classification of varied complexities. This incorporates different sorts of support vector models like polynomial, radial basis function, linear and sigmoid. The attack classification methods include training as well as testing methods with a few data samples.

In most cases regarding the SVM, the training dataset adds a few components ("traits") together with a single class label ("target values"). The primary objective behind the SVM is to produce a model that predicts the class label of the data samples in the testing dataset that are only indicated in the components. Four sorts of kernel functions are utilized to achieve this target, which are given below.

RBF: The RBF, also termed the Gaussian kernel, is formed as:

$$k_g(p_m, p_n) = \exp(-\frac{\|p_m - p_n\|}{2\sigma^2})$$

, in which σ represents the window width

Polynomial: The polynomial measure kernel is illustrated as:

$$k_g(p_m, p_n) = (p_{m,} p_n)^{dk}$$

Linear: $k_g(p_m, p_n) = p_m^{\ T} P_n$

Sigmoid: $k_g(p_m, p_n) = \tanh(k_g(p_{m,} p_n) + u)$ is termed the sigmoid kernel

In order to achieve a higher degree of accuracy in classification, the proposed framework makes use of the radial basis function to classify attacks. The classifier algorithm distinguishes the attacks based on the scope of previously identified attacks. On the off chance that the received characteristics do not match previously classified attacks, it creates a new attack category.

F. Honeypot System

The honeypot framework is a server that transmits irrelevant information to the attacker based on the attack type. This works according to the concept that "all network traffic coming to the honeypot is suspicious". The honeypot framework is located within the Demilitarized Zone. This, in turn, signifies that the original server is invisible or hidden from the intruders. By and large, the honeypot framework is created to watch the attacker's movement, store log files, and record functions similar to processes started and file additions, modifications and deletions. Thus, by gathering such details, the honeypot framework increases the total security system of the firm.

If sufficient data are gathered then they ought to be utilized to act in serious situations. These data are utilized in order to determine the attackers' skill level and identify their intention. Consequently, in terms of the attacker category, the honeypot framework sends irrelevant or fake data to the intruder. A honeypot framework is a framework designed to learn how "black-hats" probe for and exploit shortcomings in IT frameworks. It can be defined as a data framework resource whose value lies in the unapproved or illegal utilization of the asset that can be utilized for creation.

7.6 RESULTS AND DISCUSSION

In order to evaluate the proposed framework's performance, a series of investigations was performed on the extracted dataset.

Table 7.1: Attack classifications

Sl. No	Attack Classification	Attack sorts
1	R2L	15
2	DOS	10
3	Probing	6
4	U2R	7

7.6.1 Database description and types of attacks:

The Enhanced Intrusion Detection Prevention System's (EIDPS) viability was evaluated with the utilization of the KDD dataset. The KDD dataset was utilized in order to identify the attack classifications as well as to keep assailants out. Table 7.1 demonstrates a few attack types as well as the categories that are used in this research work. The attack categories, together with their types, are portrayed below:

R2L: imap, ftp-write, named, guess password, spy, send mail, snmp guess, snmp get attack, worm, phf.

DOS: land, apacha2, back, tear drop, pod, process table, smurf, udpstorm, mailbomb, netpune.

Probing: saint, satan, namp, msscan, portsweep

U2R: xtreme, perl, rootkit, sqlattack, buffer over flow, load module, httprunnel.

7.6.2 Performance Evaluation

Overhead Evaluation

Figure 7.5 outlines the overhead evaluation of the EIDPS framework. This framework uses the minimum amount of CPU assets in order to execute a lot of requests as well as response functions.

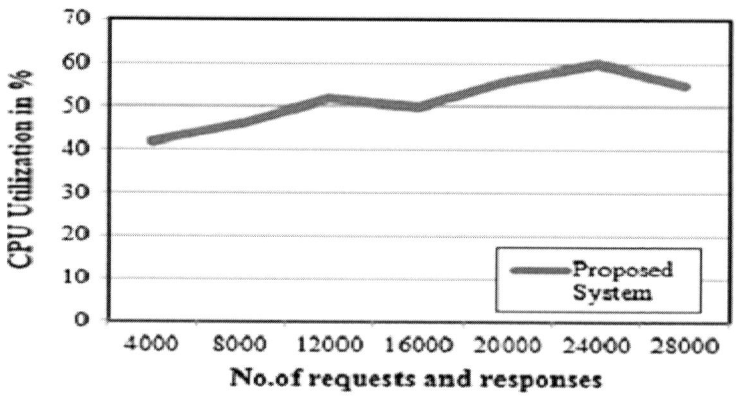

Figure 7.5: CPU utilization of the proposed framework

This illustrates the attack detection and compromising (when an attacker or malicious network traffic is identified, the response sent to the attacker or the malicious network traffic of the EIDPS is dropped). Thus, for the attack detection function, the framework uses an SVM classification calculation; Snort IDS and IDS are utilized for packet analysis, and the honeypot framework was utilized for compromising attacks. The above-mentioned algorithms enhance the performance of the proposed framework.

7.6.3 Proposed System Overall Performance

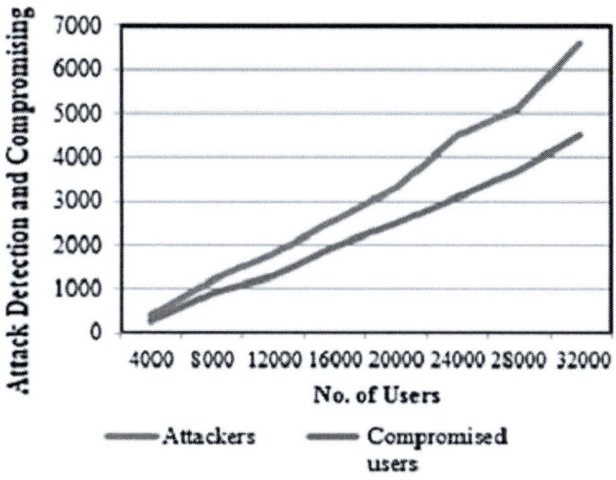

Figure 7.6: Attack detection and process compromising

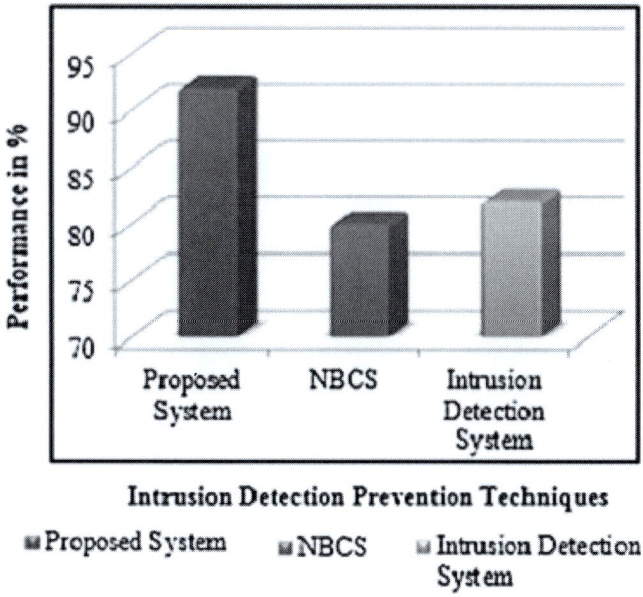

Figure 7.7: Performance evaluation of EIDPS versus Naive Bayes Classification and Intrusion Detection System frameworks

Figures 7.6 and 7.7 look at the performance of the EIDPS as well as traditional system security techniques: the Naive Bayes Attack Classification system and the IDS. In the comparison process, our EIDPS achieves maximum performance in terms of the fact that our framework uses an attack classification framework, an IPS and the honeypot system.

7.7 SUMMARY

The network environment is developing quickly and it is also generating more complex configurations of NIPS. These days, new intrusion detection systems are required to avoid intruders accessing private information. Because of this, we have introduced a new system security application known as the EIDPS. The framework provides efficient security for approved clients, aided by the support of Sebek, Snort as well as Dionaea. Similarly, it gives an attack classification, thus utilizing the Support Vector Machine classification, and an intrusion detection prevention system was utilized in order to keep away attacks, malicious code and packet analysis. Then, in order to compromise the attackers, the honeypot framework was used. Finally, our framework provides efficient security to licensed clients and prevents system intrusions in the network. Future work will concentrate on the exactness and accuracy of our algorithm in view of behavior-based prevention, which is research that can be carried out by using the dataset of actual traffic in the network.

CHAPTER 8

AN EFFECTIVE ODAIDS-HPS APPROACH FOR PREVENTING, DETECTING AND RESPONDING TO DDOS ATTACKS

8.1 INTRODUCTION

The world of computers and their interactions has been redefined by the Internet. Nowadays the entire world uses the Internet for basically everything. In regular day to day existence, it changes methods of interactions, types of business functions, interactions with organizations and the completion of everyday operations (Fathinavid & Aghababa 2012). Web services have been rolled out to all the traditional services as well, such as banking, medicine, etc.

The exponential rate of increase of interconnections relies on firms', governments' and individuals' Internet usage (Cheng *et al.* 2011). The appearance of a secure system is important to maintain the protection and security of different sites working over the web. These days, network attack (assault) prevention is one of the most discussed themes in the worldwide Internet market. Also, one of the fundamental dangers generated against the PC network are attacks that deny any service supplied to validated users and clients. Distributed Denial of Service (DDoS) assaults are launched by a vast set of machines (zombies), and the assault (attack) is carried out by a set of servers or by a unique server (Ravale *et al.* 2015).

Different applications are employed in different sorts of attacks, so it is difficult to recognize a single border firewall or IDS, since every device is only prepared to handle a specific local boundary or zone. The web server is secured, although the existing network is excessively constrained, making it impossible to have a complete picture of attacks occurring at different sites around the entire world. Internet providers and clients need to know about the wide variety of DDoS attack classifications, which was introduced by Park *et al.* (2010).

Attacks largely take one of two structures. The initial structure is designed to exploit software, where malformed packets are sent to identify the susceptibilities of the target and crash it. Vulnerable hosts are usually those that are running no antivirus program or an out-of-date antivirus program, or one which has not been appropriately patched. The second type of DDoS attack tries to deplete the victim's resources.

The attacks incorporate network bandwidth, disk space, CPU time, data structures, network connections, etc. and are consumed by different resources. It is easier to defend against the first type of attack, which is exposed by some objective, than the second form of assault, which is not able to be defended against in an easy manner. The objective of the attack could be anything or anybody, since the Internet connects the entire world (Liu & Yu 2008). Be that as it may, these sorts of loopholes in systems must be plugged to protect against malicious entities.

Thus, a new integrated intrusion detection system is proposed, and it is called the Outlier Detection Approach-based Intrusion Detection Honeypot System. It is utilized to identify, protect and respond to different DDoS assaults. The system incorporates three stages: DDoS detection, DDoS prevention, and response to DDoS attackers.

The initial two stages are resolved by the intrusion detection system utilizing the outlier detection approach to recognize malicious data that are received from unauthorized users. The transfer of data is coordinated by all trained datasets. If the error is maximized between the received network data and the trained datasets, then the data might be considered to harbor malignant data. In the third stage, the honeypot framework is utilized to send false data to unauthorized users. Additionally, it is utilized to save data about the zombies, i.e. the attackers.

8.2 DENIAL OF SERVICE

A Denial of Service (DoS) assault is basically carried out by a massive number of systems attacking a precise defect. A network attack is predictable as a Botnet attack. A Botnet comprises an enormous number of slave systems, typically termed 'zombies'. The attacked systems are frequently measured and managed by the attacker, who consumes the compromised resources.

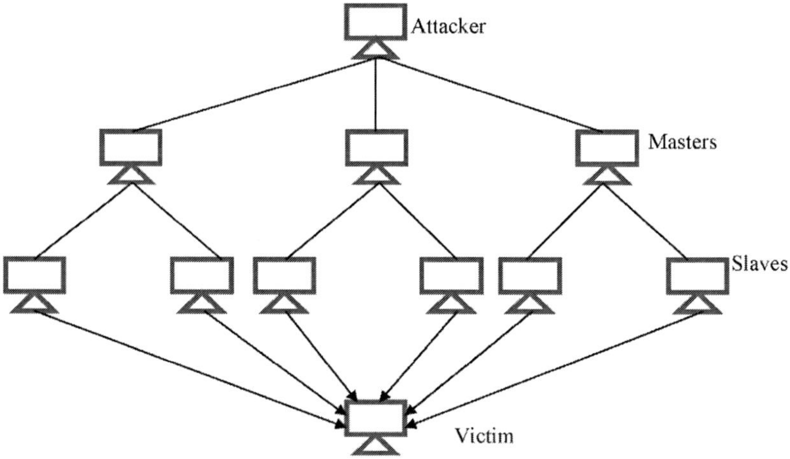

Figure 8.1: Master-Slave Architecture of a DoS Attack

A general classification of this assault includes two sorts of attacks. The first is to assault the client and not allow him/her to operate the system. The second is to attack the aforementioned server. The last added threat attacks a huge number of authorized clients per impact that are flooded without assistance.

8.3 MOTIVATION

The aim of the proposed work is to handle the attacks in an efficient way. In order to carry this out, the ODAIDS approach proposes an attack classification system. This attack classification system discovers the sorts of attacks by efficiently applying dataset components and outliers' values. In the end, the categorized results are transferred to a proposed honeypot framework, whose nodes attack an efficient system.

8.4 TYPES OF DDoS ATTACKS

There are several classes of Distributed Denial of Service attacks that disrupt a normal system. Attack tactics are divided into two techniques. The first floods the service, not allowing enough data to be transmitted for the intended validated packet data transfer. This might equally be called flooding. The second tactic is an intrusion into the hardware or programming software, making its usage impracticable.

Internet servers, routing devices, and DNS search servers are the primary targets that are interrupted at the time of an attack. This approach has both discovered the attack scenarios and identified their features. Below are essential attack techniques that have been utilized to date (Li *et al.* 2008).

8.4.1 Smurf attack

This application operates by flooding the bandwidth with defective data transfers. In this technique, the attacker sends a large number of ICMP packets to the receiver's address.

8.4.2 Ping Flood and Ping of Death

Ping floods are like smurf attacks, in which the flaw is consolidated as more ping packets are sent. The ping of death transmits corrupted packets that might destroy a system (Dhakne & Chatur 2015). Smurf and ping assaults can be sent anywhere and are difficult to defend against, as any new attacker can fix them effortlessly. There are sufficient successful defense applications against smurf and ping attacks. In any case, these attacks could create a notable defect in very small Local Area Networks (LANs).

8.4.3 TCP SYN Flood

The previous techniques operate by taking the bandwidth space into account, while this attack works by assaulting the system's CPU memory. The host tree points everything in the direction of the interface through a server's complex three-way handshake protocol before any unique data exchange occurs. The first host sends an SYN packet to start the handshake. The server responds with an acknowledgment packet. Finally, the host sends another SYN-ACK packet to maintain an efficient link. Be that as it may, attackers allow the handshake to remain half-open by not sending the last SYN. At the point at which there are a huge number of half-open associations, the server is overloaded and drops victims and memory. It will not have the capacity to serve legitimate users as its memory is ruined by false information packets (Jabez & Muthukumar 2015).

8.4.4 UDP Flood

A UDP flood is like a ping flood. Like ping parcels, UDP packets besiege the server. UDP may well be significantly more efficient than ICMP for a few systems due to the size of the UDP packets being much larger. The packet can fit in 65000 bytes without difficulty, and it floods specific ethernet systems as soon as various zombies are set up.

8.5 DDoS ATTACK OVERVIEW

A Denial of Service (DoS) attack is described as an external attempt by attackers to prevent the authentic utilization of services (Keung *et al.* 2010). A Distributed Denial of Service (DDoS) assault uses different approaches to accomplish this objective. There are numerous approaches to execute a DoS attack. One of the possible approaches for the assailant is to send a flood of packets to an intruder; this stream uses up some key resources, thereby rendering it inaccessible to the interrupted authorized user. An additional basic approach is for the attacker to send a couple of distorted packets to generate confusion for an application or protocol running on the interrupted machine, then compel it to freeze or to boot up. There is an onset of attacks that over-burden the network's implementation instead of focusing on particular defects.

Yet another conceivable approach is to refuse access to necessary components of the defected network, then use up several key resources so authorized users of the same system cannot access the internal or external system. This list is a long way from being comprehensive. There are numerous different approaches that attack services on the Internet that we cannot anticipate, and these may only be found after they have been utilized in a vast assault. While trying to better comprehend DoS attacks, this section will proceed to answer the following questions: (1) what makes DDoS attacks possible, and (2) what is the assailant's motivation?

8.5.1 DDoS Attack Strategies

A Distributed Denial of Service (DDoS) attack is carried out in a few stages. The attacker first enlists different operator (slave) machines. This procedure is typically performed by looking for remote machines and searching for security openings that will empower subversion. Defected machines are then abused by utilizing the identified defects and are influenced by the assault code. The defective/influenced stage is also mechanized, and influenced machines are utilized through the addition of novel agents.

The agent's machine is utilized to send assault packets. An attacker has basically enveloped the identity of the undermined machines at the time of the attack through determining the basic address field in the assault packet. Nonetheless, this determination is not generally essential for an effective DDoS attack. Except for reflector assaults, all other attack types utilize spoofing just to prevent the location of the attack and the identification of agent machines from becoming known.

8.6 INTERNET ARCHITECTURE OF DDoS

The Internet was organized on insecure processes and it has been extremely effective in achieving its objectives. It offers users fast, straightforward and low expense correspondence and applications, which are upheld with different large-level protocols that guarantee an efficient or time-based transmission of communications or a specific level of QoS. Subsequently, the Internet plan has utilized end-to-end parameters: the interaction end hosts direct multifaceted functionalities to achieve selected administration validations, while the intermediate system is stretched to the bare-minimum, best-effort management of essentially sending packets from the source to the destination. The Internet is supervised in a distributed way along these lines, and there is no common strategy that is upheld between its users. The Internet framework thus creates rare security issues concerning the probabilities for DDoS attacks:

1. Web security is more inter-related: DDoS attacks are usually received from systems that are directed through security-related approaches. Notwithstanding how secure the victim's system might be, its defenselessness against DDoS assaults depends on the state of the security of the wider world wide web (Wang *et al.* 2011).

2. Web resources are restricted: Each Internet element (network, host, service) restricts its resources from being overloaded due to an excessive amount of users.

3. The force of the many is more powerful than the force of the few. Facilitated and collaborative malicious actions by less significant members will regularly inconvenience others if the resources of the attackers are more prominent than those of the victims.

4. Accountability is not implemented. In IP packets, the source delivery field is expected to convey the IP address of the machine, which gets initiated from a packet. If the suspicion is not approved or otherwise upheld at any time between the source and the goal, it creates a chance for source address spoofing, generating a duplicate of the source address field in the packet. Source address spoofing bounces from aggressors' capable systems to outsource responsibility for their events and sometimes it triggers the way attacks are executed, for example, reflector attacks and smurf attacks (Vamsi & Kant 2015).

5. Control is distributed. Web administration is distributed, and every system is kept running according to local strategies characterized by its owners. The consequences of this are numerous. There is no real way to uphold a worldwide organization of a specific security system or security approach, and because of security concerns, it is frequently difficult to examine cross-network activity behavior.

8.6.1 DDoS Defense Challenges

The seriousness of the DDoS issue and the maximized frequency, complexity and quality of assaults have prompted various security system approaches. However, although it has been more than three years since the initially appropriated assaults were executed, since when numerous arrangements have been created, the issue has scarcely been handled as it cannot be solved individually.

1. Requirement for distributed response at numerous points: The previous sections have explained how there are numerous conceivable DDoS attacks, few of which can be maintained only by the detected node. It is therefore important to distribute a potentially organized response framework. Additionally, it is crucial that a focused response is sent across the Internet to protect against different operators and victims from being selected.

2. Absence of detailed attack data

It is generally accepted that reporting the events of assaults harms the business routines of the intruded networks. In this manner, the data that exist about different attacks are exceptionally restricted, and attacks are only accounted for by government bodies with a commitment to keeping them secret. It is hard to outline creative answers for the issue if one cannot get comfortable with it. The attack data are sometimes mistaken for attack device data, which are freely accessible at numerous Internet destinations. Attack data include the attack type, the time and form of the attack, attempted responses and its viability, threats, etc.

3. Absence of security system benchmarks: Numerous sellers take intense care that their solution totally handles the DDoS issue. There is as of now no benchmark suite of attack situations that would empower an examination between security systems. Such a circumstance is probably going to discourage networks from investing resources in DDoS protection, since there are no guarantees about the nature of the item being purchased.

4. Trouble of vast scale testing

DDoS defenses should be tried in a reasonable situation. This is as of now incomprehensible because of the absence of extensive scale test-beds, safe approaches to perform live distributed attempts over the Internet, or point by point and sensible simulation devices that can help a small or a large number of nodes. Assertions about security system performance are consequently made in terms of small-scale trials and simulations, and are not credible.

8.7 OVERVIEW

8.7.1 ODAIDS-HPS SYSTEM

DDoS attacks are divided into three classifications: volume-based attacks, which incorporate ICMP floods as well as spoofed packet floods; protocol attacks, where the resources of a genuine server are consumed by the attack, and which essentially include ping of death, STN floods, DDoS floods, and fragmented packet attacks; and zero-day DDoS attacks, the objective of which is a moderate crash of the web server. DDoS assaults can be avoided by means of utilizing the proposed ODAIDS-HPS framework.

Figure 8.1 demonstrates the proposed network framework structure, which has three imperative parts that are utilized in the handling of DDoS assaults: the outlier detection-based IDS, the attack classifier, and the honeypot system. Original servers are accessed from an approved client utilizing legitimate data by means of an ODA-based IDS. Actual servers are overloaded through the attacker's agent; subsequently, agents are system or software applications. An actual server's resources are possessed by operators with the aid of malicious data.

8.7.2 Outlier Detection-Based IDS

Another outlier discovery technique that appears in Figure 8.2 is the proposed intrusion detection system; furthermore, the proposed technique recognizes intrusion attacks from the computer network. The proposed IDS demands a set of absolutely typical data in order to prepare the model. An Internet Service Provider (ISP) gives an ordinary dataset for this, which is created by unconventional strategies. Earlier recognition models are considered outliers in this technique. The remaining data outliers are considered as altogether different data points, and the estimation is taken with some parameters that are computer-based. Using a dataset, the outlier approach works productively and manages anomaly detection.

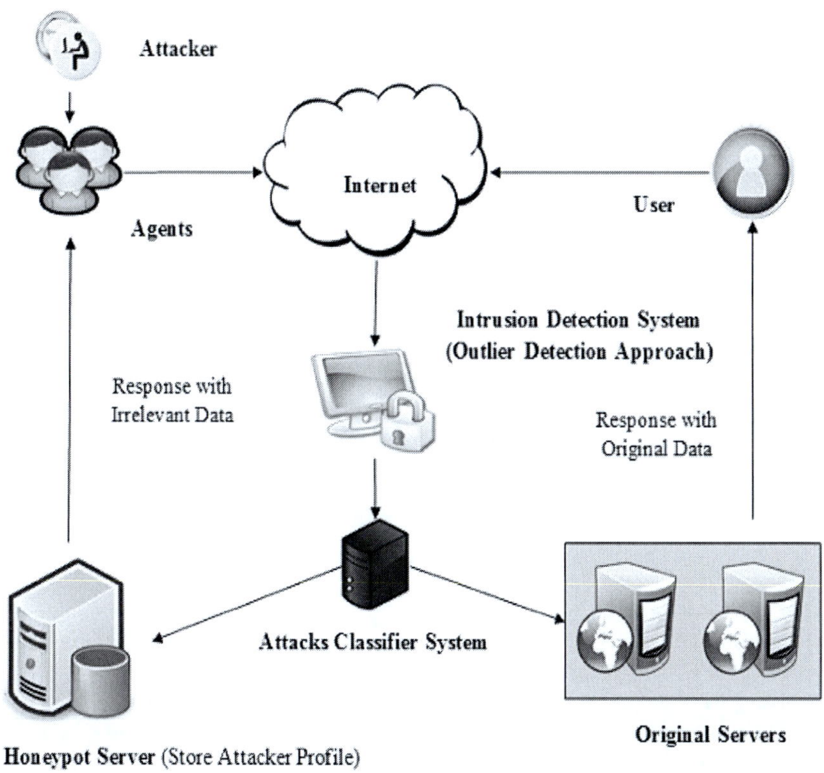

Figure 8.2: Proposed network architecture

Consider a data packet (P) that incorporates various attributes ($A_1, A_2 \ldots A_n$). Likewise, data packet P can be arranged into types, for example, trained data packet Ψ_p or test data packet Φ_p. An outlier value of the test data packet Φ_p can be figured out by using the following formula.

$$o\left(\phi_p\right) = \sum_{i=1}^{n} \sqrt{(\psi_{Ai}) - (\Phi_{Ai})}^2$$

The proposed estimation depends on the distance of the kth nearest neighbor from point O. Consider that k and point O are given, then $D^k(O)$ signifies the distance from point O towards the kth closest neighbor. So the distance

(O) is a measure of the outlierness of case O. The points with larger $D^k(O)$ values have more sparsely distributed neighborhoods and represent powerful outliers, and points belonging to a place with dense clusters have lower values for $D^k(O)$. The user will have an interest in the top n anomalies for this technique. This method characterizes an outlier as follows: given a k as well as an n, location O can be considered as an outlier if the distance to the kth closest neighbor is lower than the corresponding values for no more than (n-1) other points.

The top n outliers with the maximized $D^k(O)$ qualities are considered outliers. So the previous steps alter the proposed outlier identification scheme when k = 1. The "outlier threshold" will subsequently be utilized to evaluate if it is an outlier or not. About 2% is utilized as a threshold for training data. To evaluate the threshold, distances for all data points from training data (e.g. "ordinary behavior" data) to their closest neighbors are computed and after that are sorted. Outliers are recognized by the threshold distance of the data points to their closest neighbors.

8.7.3 Attack Classifier

The proposed framework is imperative for discovering the sort of attack that appears in Figure 8.3. To sort the DDoS attacks, the outlier must evaluate the values and dataset components of received network packets utilizing the proposed IDS. An IDS distinguishes received packets as anomalies or normal by utilizing the computed outlier values. A feature of the system activity is that the "rate of associations has the same destination host and the same service" as well as the same packet-level features.

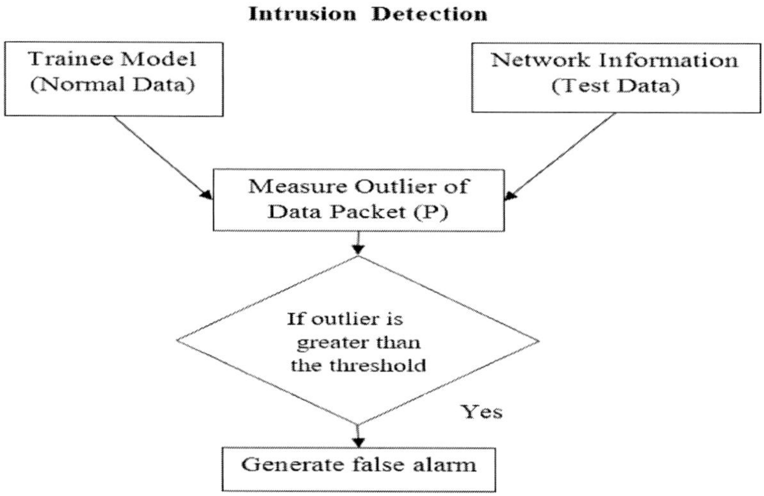

Figure 8.3: Outlier detection approach-based IDS

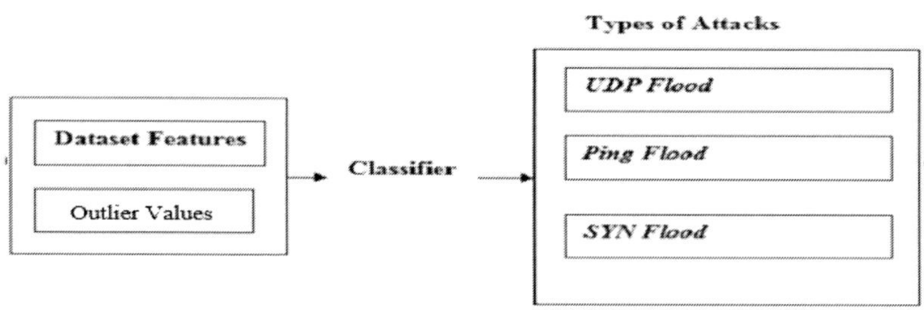

Figure 8.4: Classification of Attacks

8.7.4 Honeypot System

This framework is characterized as a "decoy" framework that will not maintain the operating system or make resources easy to access. A decoy framework should carry various fake files, directories and other information that appear to be genuine. Honeypots ought to persuade the programmer that he has accessed critical data and seem, by all accounts, to be a legitimate machine with legitimate files.

It will then trick the intruders so that the genuine information that is vulnerable can be accessed. The proposed work will resolve the issue by utilizing the honeypot with an IDS. It is not used for coordinating or routing traffic, but rather to compromise. Data capture and analysis are utilized to lessen the stream of production traffic. The proposed honeypot catches unapproved activity utilized for hacking purposes. The framework decreases traffic production and false negatives.

Owing to limited production activity, the honeypot lessens false positives and catches anything that arrives in or leaves the network. It catches all activity that can be viewed as suspicious or can be recorded as unknown, even when the IDS and the system fail to distinguish an activity. It can review all the activities to recognize an attack, then react to the attack by sending irrelevant information. The planning and mitigation data responses to DDoS assaults are clarified by Salehian *et al.* (2010).

8.8 RESULTS AND DISCUSSION

The outlier detection technique has a tendency to calculate the outlier values of the traffic in the given time period. At the point that a DDoS flooding-based attack occurs, the outlier detection strategy uses the features of IP packets that incorporate a set of attributes and features, and similar size IP packets are utilized in defiance of the victim's response.

Network traffic will happen because of the particular packet size, with respect to requests as well as responses, data flood, and acknowledgments. The more focused size distribution of IP packets has a small entropy measure, and the more dispersed size distribution of IP packets has a bigger entropy measure. This technique offers access to legitimate clients and the source IP address to keep away attacks from zombies. In estimating entropy with outlier values, the source IP address is changed and chooses where traffic happens and where it is discarded.

When the IDS framework identifies an IP address as a malicious address, it forwards the IP packet information to the attack classifier. At that point, the classifier orders the received packets into specific classifications of attacks based on packet characteristics and outlier values. These are sent to the proposed honeypot framework. The honeypot framework stores the results in the database then reacts to the malicious client with false or deceiving data. Additionally, current honeypot frameworks (Wang *et al.* 2011) do not ensure better results than the proposed framework. The results proposed through the technique are demonstrated below.

Table 8.1: Set of features used by the proposed IDS

1	Duration	13	Host login
2	Protocol type	14	Guest login
3	Service	15	Send error rate
4	Flag	16	Service send error rate
5	Source bytes	17	Received error rate
6	Destination bytes	18	Same service rate
7	Number of failed logins	19	Service different host rate
8	Service received	20	Destination host service count
9	Error rate	21	Destination host at different service rate
10	Service rate	22	Destination host service at different host rate
11	Destination host count	23	Destination host service send error rate
12	Logged in	24	Destination host service received error rate

Table 8.1 demonstrates various factors that are used in the proposed IDS for DDoS attacks with the gathered network data. These components play an essential part in the detection of assailants in secure system communication. In the event that any changes happen to these components, the distances of the datasets, as well as the outlier values, will be affected.

Table 8.2: Fragmentation of a trained normal dataset

ID	Duration	Flag	Source byte	Destination byte
1	81	18	522	0
2	12	61	0	0
3	22	61	0	0
4	65	184	520	0
5	45	47	0	0
6	66	28	522	0
7	78	132	18	0
8	45	134	0	0
9	74	58	89	0
10	35	1	50	0

Table 8.2 demonstrates the fragmented details of the trained normal dataset. The datasets are gathered from different network communication levels with different internet service provider strategies, due to the fact that one internet service supplier's approach can vary from another.

Table 8.3: Fragmentation of information received from various users

ID	Duration	Flag	Source byte	Destination byte
1	10	SF	491	0
2	22	334	0	0
3	56	146	0	0
4	78	199	420	0
5	66	28	0	0
6	98	233	616	0
7	569	147	105	0
8	45	RSTR	0	0
9	87	255	861	0
10	35	1	0	0

Table 8.3 demonstrates partial data about the network data that are received from different clients. The network data may vary from client to client as a result of the fact that every client utilizes a different internet service provider. Table 8.4 demonstrates the distance as well as the outlier values that are evaluated by our proposed outlier detection approach.

Table 8.4: Distance and outlier values of tested data

ID	Distance	Outlier Value
1	2.4	5
2	4.5	8
3	3.5	7
4	5.5	10
5	2.3	4
6	1.1	2
7	2.6	3
8	4.1	4
9	2.6	3
10	2.8	5

Figure 8.5 demonstrates DDoS attack detections carried out over the course of a month. The graph demonstrates a correlation between the total number of assaults identified each day on a home-based system and the number of assaults that are really redirected by our approach. The chart demonstrates that almost 80% of the attacks occurred as predicted in advance. A reliable outlier detection approach strategy is shown in Figure 8.6. The approach effectively achieved the task and almost 80% of system attacks were redirected, with a standard deviation of 8.379%.

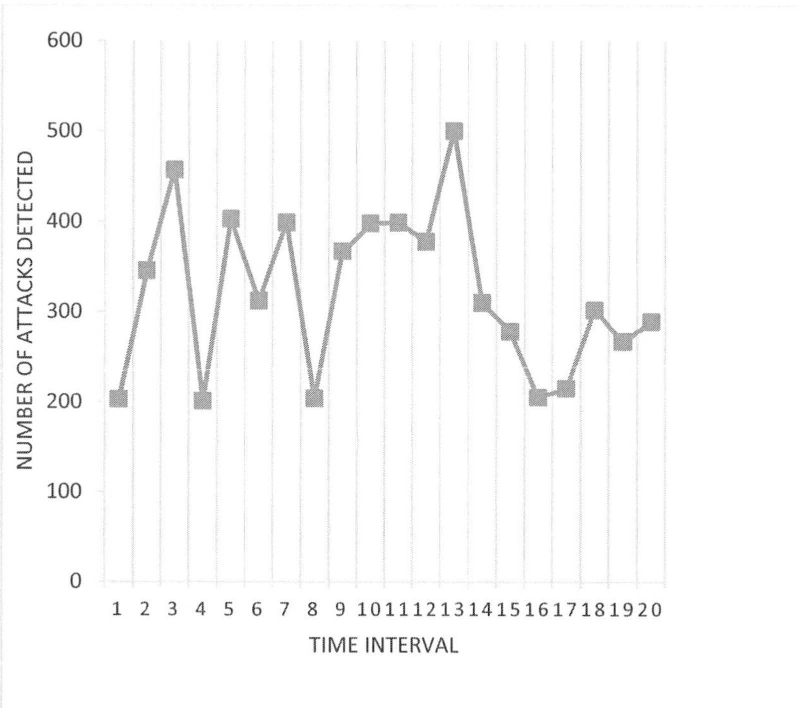

Figure 8.5: Total attacks detected versus actual attacks redirected to honeypot system

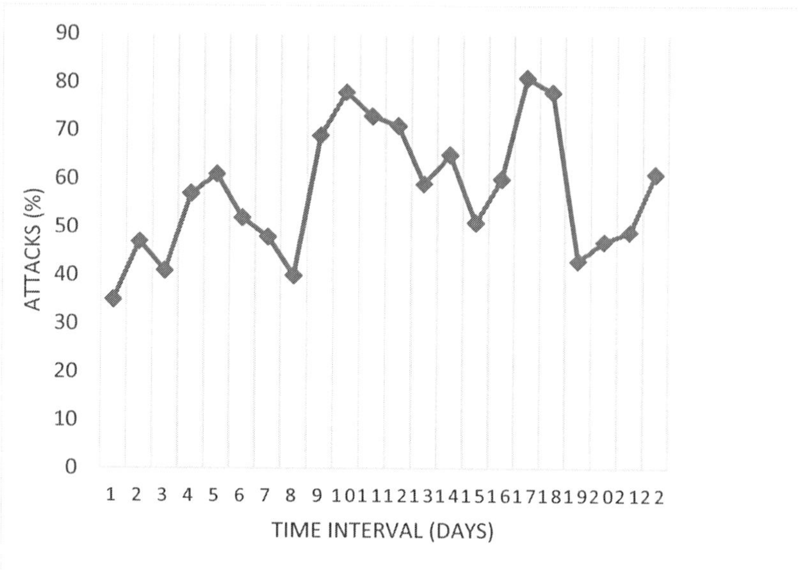

Figure 8.6: Percent of attacks detected and redirected by proposed framework

Table 8.5: Honeypot compromised users after various time intervals

ID	Total web server access	Compromised users	Allowed users
1	5000	2333	2667
2	6600	2300	4300
3	8000	3000	5000
4	20000	4500	15500
5	25000	5000	20000

The above demonstrates an outlier quality that may maximize the uncertainty of the distance between an ordinary and a verified dataset. Table 8.5 demonstrates the total resources received from the transferred web server. It shows an extreme number of attackers who are compromised when the sent honeypot framework is not an actual server. A honeypot framework responds to compromise the client with different amounts of false data in view of their behavior.

8.9 SUMMARY

Intrusion detection and responding to DDoS attacks on interconnected computer systems are common goals of system security. Consequently, the information produced from traffic monitoring in the network includes high dimensionality, volume, and heterogeneity. The parameters plus the overall mining algorithm are not suitable at the time of the occurrence of more than one low-frequency network assault. Furthermore, cyber-attacks can be created from different sorts of locations as well, and can also aim for dissimilar types of machines. Thus a strategy is needed to examine these sorts of network data. Our ODAIDS approach documented those categories of disruptions successfully, after which the intrusion features were forwarded to the proposed attack classifier framework. This identified the sorts of attacks productively, utilizing dataset components and outlier values. At that point, the characterized result was sent to the proposed honeypot framework that handled the assaults efficiently. In the future, we hope to design an entire intrusion detection system that will detect and cancel all attacks against all computer threats. However, this proposed framework detects more computer threats compared to less effective intrusion detection systems.

CHAPTER 9

CONCLUSIONS AND FUTURE WORK

Chapter 1 provided a brief introduction about intrusion detection techniques and approaches, and the techniques involved were also explained in the following chapters. Finally, an overview of the work as well as its organization was proposed, indicating how each chapter corresponds to the proposed techniques.

Chapter 2 described the background study of the work. This was discussed in order to understand the basic concepts. This was of help while developing the proposed mechanisms.

Chapter 3 examined the existing work on the newly proposed techniques and discussed them briefly. While researching the current system, the restrictions of prevailing protocols were studied and provided inspiration to develop a new process. The evaluation considered all weaknesses detected in the present system.

Chapter 4 was focused on the honeypot and the intrusion detection system. Honeypots were, to a great extent, what were utilized for the prevention and detection of attacks that diminish security measures and for converting the framework into a more proficient system for the estimation of security functions. The honeypot utilization mechanism directly implements security mechanisms, thus securing the system from attackers. Basically, a honeypot is a system that gathers and records information about the data. Its major drawback is that it is not possible to detect the black-hat attackers or establish tasks towards them. Additionally, the chapter established that the major aim is to detect attackers and hackers as well as to gather information about them.

Chapter 5 examined the ant-based DDOS technique utilizing roaming virtual honeypots (ADTRVH). Here, the virtual roaming honeypot was utilized, aided by a multi-level protection model, in order to group the data with regard to different intruders at various levels in the system. In view of the ACO method, the gathered data were transmitted to several layers of the security model, thus diminishing the number of honeypot intruders as well as avoiding the distribution of intruders. The MLIP identifies system intruders to various degrees. After the identification of the affected domain, information is transmitted to various levels in order to eliminate the contiguous distribution of attacks to the honeypot framework by establishing a defense framework over the attackers. It illustrated that the newly introduced methodology diminished the ratio of packet delivery and minimized false positives.

Chapter 6 described the intrusions as well as attacks avoided by utilizing the proposed FPSIDS-HPS approach. That proposed framework structure has five main parts to handle in order to avoid different network intrusions: FPS, LB, MS, TV and honeypot systems. 1) The original user is initially connected with the web and then communicates with the FPS, which first checks the user's status then forwards it to the LB. 2) The LB creates the token keys used for the user as well as the attacker that is intruding on the system.

The LB produces two different token keys with various ranges. The LB forwards the generated token keys to the MS. 3) The MS receives the token keys of the user/attacker separately. At whatever point the user/attacker gets the token key, it is directed to the token key verifier. 4) The TV confirms the received token range; if the received token is from the unique user, then the received token is legitimate. At that point, the TV forwards demands to the unique server, and likewise the server sends the respective information to the comparing client. Otherwise, the token key is sent through the attacker and the gained token range remains distinctive. Therefore, the request ought to be forwarded to the honeypot framework. 5) Finally, the honeypot framework sends irrelevant information to the attacker. Honeypots give out huge IDSs that can be utilized to figure out whether a computer network or server has encountered an unapproved intrusion.

Chapter 7 described the EIDPS, an efficient approach for network protection and intrusion prevention. Thus, the enhanced interruption detection prevention system was proposed to avoid intrusions. Attackers are classified by utilizing the intrusion detection prevention system. With the help of the proposed approach, efficient security throughout the entire network is achieved, thus avoiding the unknown third party attackers. Our framework gives ongoing security to licensed clients, aided by Sebek, Snort and Dionaea. This likewise gives a classification of attacks by utilizing the SVM (Support Vector Machine) specification, as well as keeping away intrusions and malicious code, and we used the intrusion detection prevention system for the identification of packets. At that point, a honeypot framework was used to respond to the attackers. Finally, our framework gives efficient security to licensed clients and in addition keeps the system intrusion within the network.

Chapter 8 verified an efficient ODAIDS-HPS mechanism aimed at responding to, preventing and detecting DDoS attacks. The aim was to handle the attacks in an efficient way. In order to maintain this, the ODAIDS approach planned an attack classifier framework. This framework efficiently distinguishes between categories of assaults by employing dataset components as well as outlier values. The classified results are referred to the proposed honeypot framework, which is an efficient technique against the attacks.

Identifying intrusions and responding to DDoS assaults against computer frameworks is the overall task of system security. Moreover, cyber assaults can be created from different sorts of locations and, furthermore, they can target different machines. Accordingly, a strategy is needed to detect different types of system information. The ODAIDS approach is familiar with such sorts of disruptions, and afterward the intrusion's points of interest are sent to the proposed attack classifier framework. Then the attack classifier framework identifies the types of attacks efficiently, applying dataset components and outlier values. At that point, the classified data are sent to our proposed honeypot framework that switches the attacks in an effective way.

FUTURE WORK

In the future, we would like to implement a complete intrusion detection system that will identify and invalidate all attacks against all computer threats. However, the proposed framework is more effective at detecting computer threats than less proficient intrusion detection techniques.

REFERENCES

Abduvaliyev, A., Pathan, A. S. K., Zhou, J., Roman, R., & Wong, W. C. (2013). On the vital areas of intrusion detection systems in wireless sensor networks. *IEEE Communications Surveys & Tutorials*, *15*(3), 1223-1237.

Acharya, R., & Asha, K. (2008). Data integrity and intrusion detection in wireless sensor networks. In *16th IEEE Int. Conf. on Networks* (pp. 1-5). IEEE.

Ahmed, A. S., & Rajeswari, A. (2012). Intrusion detection in heterogeneous Wireless Sensor Networks with an energy efficient localization algorithm. In *Int. Conf. on ICRTIT* (pp. 389-394). IEEE.

Aka, P (2018). E-MAIL SERVER USING THREADED SOCKETS. Afribary.com: Retrieved March 29, 2019, from https://afribary.com/works/e-mail-server-using-threaded-sockets-8410

Andreolini, M., Colajanni, M. & Marchetti, M. (2014). A collaborative framework for intrusion detection in mobile 4 networks. *Information Sciences*, *6*, 1-4.

Bao, F., Chen, R., Chang, M., & Cho, J. H. (2011). Trust-based intrusion detection in wireless sensor networks. *2011 IEEE International Conference on Conference Communications (ICC)* (pp. 1-6). IEEE.

Bao, F., Chen, R., Chang, M., & Cho, J. H. (2012). Hierarchical trust management for wireless sensor networks and its applications to trust-based routing and intrusion detection. *IEEE transactions on network and service management*, *9*(2), 169-183.

Butun, I., Morgera, S. D., & Sankar, R. (2014). A survey of intrusion detection systems in wireless sensor networks. *IEEE communications surveys & tutorials*, *16*(1), 266-282.

Cárdenas, A. A., Berthier, R., Bobba, R. B., Huh, J. H., Jetcheva, J. G., Grochocki, D., & Sanders, W. H. (2014). A framework for evaluating intrusion detection architectures in advanced metering infrastructures. *IEEE Transactions on Smart Grid*, *5*(2), 906-915.

Chappidi, S. R., Kuthadi, V. M., (2017). Differentiated Service Model for Best Effort Packet Delivery in Advanced Wireless Networks. *International Journal of Advanced Engineering and Global Technology*, *5*(1), 1502-1508.

Cheng, C. T., Chi, K. T., & Lau, F. C. (2011). A delay-aware data collection network structure for wireless sensor networks. *IEEE Sensors Journal*, *11*(3), 699-710.

Chen, J., Li, J., & Lai, T. H. (2013). Energy-efficient intrusion detection with a barrier of probabilistic sensors: Global and local. *IEEE Transactions on Wireless Communications*, *12*(9), 4742-4755.

Coppolino, L., D'Antonio, S., Romano, L., & Spagnuolo, G. (2010). An intrusion detection system for critical information infrastructures using wireless sensor network technologies. In *5th Int. Conf. on CRIS* (pp. 1-8). IEEE.

Coppolino, L., D'Antonio, S., Garofalo, A. & Romano, L. (2013). Applying Data Mining Techniques to Intrusion Detection in Wireless Sensor Networks. In *2013 Eighth International Conference on P2P, Parallel, Grid, Cloud and Internet Computing*. IEEE.

Dhakne, A. R., & Chatur, P. N. (2015). Distributed Trust based Intrusion Detection approach in wireless sensor network. In *CCI* (pp. 96-101). IEEE.

El-Alfy, E. S. M., & Al-Obeidat, F. N. (2014). A multicriterion fuzzy classification method with greedy attribute selection for anomaly-based intrusion detection. *Procedia Computer Science*, *34*, 55-62.

El-Ghali, M. and Masri, W. (2009). Intrusion detection using signatures extracted from execution profiles. In Proceedings of the 2009 ICSE Workshop on Software Engineering for Secure Systems (pp. 17-24). IEEE Computer Society.

Estiri, M., & Khademzadeh, A. (2010). A theoretical signaling game model for intrusion detection in wireless sensor networks. In *14th International NETWORKS* (pp. 1-6). IEEE.

Estiri, M. and Khademzadeh, A. (2010). A game-theoretical model for intrusion detection in wireless sensor networks. *In CCECE* 2010 (pp. 1-5). IEEE.

Fathinavid, A. H., & Aghababa, A. B. (2012). A Protocol for Intrusion Detection Based on Learning Automata in Forwarding Packets for Distributed Wireless Sensor Networks. In *Int. Conf. on Cyber* (pp. 373-380). IEEE.

Gheorghe, L., Rughinis, R., & Tataroiu, R. (2012). Adaptive Trust Management Protocol based on Intrusion Detection for Wireless Sensor Networks. *WSN*, *8*, 1-7.

Ghosal, A. and Halder, S. (2013). Intrusion detection in wireless sensor networks: Issues, challenges and approaches. In Wireless networks and security (pp. 329-367). Springer, Berlin, Heidelberg.

Guerroumi, M., Derhab, A., & Saleem, K. (2015). Intrusion Detection System against Sink Hole Attack in Wireless Sensor Networks with Mobile Sink. In *12th Int. Conf. on ITNG* (pp. 307-313). IEEE.

Guo, Q., Li, X., Feng, Z., & Xu, G. (2015). MPOID: Multi-protocol Oriented Intrusion Detection Method for Wireless Sensor Networks. *2015 IEEE 17th International Conference on High Performance Computing and Communications*. IEEE.

Hari, P. C., Babu, E. S., Rao, M. S., & Kuthadi, V. M. (2016). Implementation of Contour Based Intrusion Detection System against Black Hole Attack in Wireless Ad hoc Networks. *International Journal of Advanced Engineering and Global Technology*, *4*(1), 1736-1743.

Han, G., Jiang, J., Shen, W., Shu, L., & Rodrigues, J. (2013). IDSEP: a novel intrusion detection scheme based on energy prediction in cluster-based wireless sensor networks. *IET Information Security*, *7*(2), 97-105.

Huang, J. Y., Liao, I. E., Chung, Y. F., & Chen, K. T. (2013). Shielding wireless sensor network using Markovian intrusion detection system with attack pattern mining. *Information Sciences*, *231*, 32-44.

Idowu, R. K., Maroosi, A., Muniyandi, R. C., & Othman, Z. A. (2013). An application of membrane computing to anomaly-based intrusion detection system. *Procedia Technology*, *11*, 585-592.

Jabez, J., & Muthukumar, B. (2015). Intrusion Detection System (IDS): Anomaly detection using outlier detection approach. *Procedia Computer Science*, *48*, 338-346.

Jano M., Kunchai, Y. X., Tian L., & Wei H. (2010). High interaction Honeypot system for SQL injection analysis. *WSN*, *12*, 274-277.

Keung, Y., Li, B., & Zhang, Q. (2010). The intrusion detection in mobile sensor network. In *Proceedings of the eleventh ACM international symposium on Mobile ad hoc networking and computing* (pp. 11-20). ACM.

Krishnan, D. (2015). A distributed self-adaptive Intrusion Detection System for Mobile Ad-hoc Networks using tamper evident mobile agents. *Procedia Computer Science*, *46*, 1203-1208.

Kuthadi, V. M., Selvaraj, R., & Marwala, T. (2017). Energy Efficient Scheduling Technique for Minimizing Data Collection Delay of Multiple Sink in WSNs. *International Journal of Control Theory and Applications*, *10*(32), 393-407.

Kuthadi, V. M., & Marwala, T. (2017). Energy Efficient EMO Algorithm Based Scheduling Technique in Wireless Sensor Networks. *Asian Journal of Information Technology*, *16*(11-12), 816-824.

Kuthadi, V. M., Selvaraj, R., & Marwala, T. (2015). An efficient web services framework for secure data collection in wireless sensor networks. *British Journal of Science*, *12*(1), 18-31.

Kuthadi, V. M, Rajendra, C. & Selvaraj, R. (2010). A study of security challenges in wireless sensor networks. *JATIT*, *20*(1), 39-44.

Kuthadi V. M., Selvaraj R., & Marwala T. (2018) Energy Efficient Secure Data Transmission in Wireless Sensor Network. In S. Satapathy, V. Bhateja, & S. Das (eds.), *Smart Computing and Informatics. Smart Innovation, Systems and Technologies*, vol. 77. Singapore: Springer. DOI: 10.1007/979-981-10-5544-7_28.

Kuthadi V. M., Selvaraj R., & Marwala T. (2016) Data Size Reduction and Maximization of the Network Lifetime over Wireless Sensor Network. In S. Satapathy, J. Mandal, S. Udgata, & Bhateja V. (eds.), *Information Systems Design and Intelligent Applications. Advances in Intelligent Systems and Computing*, vol. 433. New Delhi: Springer. DOI: 10.1007/978-81-322-2755-7_75.

Kuthadi, V. M., Selvaraj, R., & Marwala, T. (2016). An Enhanced Security Pattern for Wireless Sensor Network. In *Proceedings of the Second International Conference on Computer and Communication Technologies* (pp. 61-71). New Delhi: Springer. DOI: 10.1007/978-81-322-2523-2_6.

Kuthadi, V. M., Selvaraj, R., & Marwala, T. (2015). An efficient adaptive pre-processing mechanism for streaming sensor data. In *2015 IEEE 9th International Conference on Intelligent Systems and Control (ISCO)* (pp. 1-6). IEEE. DOI:10.1109/ISCO.2015.7282266.

Lin, S. W., Ying, K. C., Lee, C. Y., & Lee, Z. J. (2012). An intelligent algorithm with feature selection and decision rules applied to anomaly intrusion detection. *Applied Soft Computing*, *12*(10), 3285-3290.

Livani, M. A., & Abadi, M. (2010). Distributed PCA-based anomaly detection in wireless sensor networks. In *International Conference for ICITST* (pp. 1-8). IEEE.

Li, G., He, J., & Fu, Y. (2008). Group-based intrusion detection system in wireless sensor networks. *Computer Communications*, *31*(18), 4324-4332.

Li, L., Li, Y. H., Fu, D. Y., & Ming, W. (2010). Intrusion detection model based on hierarchical structure in wireless sensor networks. In *Int. Conf. on ICECE* (pp. 2816-2819). IEEE.

Li, H., Pandit, V., Katneni, N., & Agrawal, D. P. (2012). A reverse Gaussian deployment strategy for intrusion detection in wireless sensor networks. In *IEEE Int. Conf. on Communications (ICC)* (pp. 6678-6682). IEEE.

Liu, Y., & Yu, F. (2008). Immunity-based intrusion detection for wireless sensor networks. In *IEEE Int. Conf. on IJCNN* (pp. 439-444). IEEE.

Medhat, K., Ramadan, R.A. and Talkhan, I.,(2017). Towards distributed layered intrusion detection system for large scale wireless sensor networks. *International Journal of Intelligent Engineering Informatics*, 5(1), pp.1-28.

Maleh, Y., Ezzati, A., Qasmaoui, Y., & Mbida, M. (2015). A global hybrid intrusion detection system for wireless sensor networks. *Procedia Computer Science*, *52*, 1047-1052.

Moosavi, H., & Bui, F. M. (2014). A game-theoretic framework for robust optimal intrusion detection in wireless sensor networks. *IEEE Transactions on Information Forensics and Security*, *9*(9), 1367-1379.
Muntjir, M., Rahul, M. and Alhumyani, H.A. (2017). An Analysis of Internet of Things (IoT): Novel Architectures, Modern Applications, Security Aspects and Future Scope with Latest Case Studies. *Int. J. Eng. Res. Technol*, *6*, pp.422-447

Park, N. H., Oh, S. H., & Lee, W. S. (2010). Anomaly intrusion detection by clustering transactional audit streams in a host computer. *Information Sciences*, *180*(12), 2375-2389.

Patel, A., Taghavi, M., Bakhtiyari, K. and JúNior, J.C. (2013). An intrusion detection and prevention system in cloud computing: A systematic review. *Journal of network and computer applications*, *36*(1), pp.25-41

Ponomarchuk, Y., & Seo, D. W. (2010). Intrusion detection based on traffic analysis in wireless sensor networks. In *19th Annual WOCC* (pp. 1-7). IEEE.

Pramod, P. J., Srikanth, S. V., Vivek, N., Patil, M. U., & Sarat, C. B. N. (2009). Intelligent intrusion detection system (In2DS) using wireless sensor networks. In *International Conference on ICNSC '09* (pp. 587-591). IEEE.

Rajkumar, D. U. S., & Vayanaperumal, R. (2015). A leader based intrusion detection system for preventing intruder in heterogeneous wireless sensor network. In *IBSS, IEEE* (pp. 1-6). IEEE.

Ranjan A., Selvaraj, R., Kuthadi V.M., & Marwala T. (2018). Stealthy Attacks in MANET to Detect and Counter Measure by Ant Colony Optimization. In A. Kalam, S. Das, & K. Sharma (eds.) *Advances in Electronics, Communication and Computing. Lecture Notes in Electrical*

Engineering, vol. 443. Singapore: Springer. DOI: 10.1007/978-981-10-4765-7_62.

Ranjan A., Kuthadi, V. M. Selvaraj, R. & Marwala, T. (2013). Detection and Avoidance of Routing Attacks in Mobile Ad-hoc Networks Using Intelligent Node. In *Proceedings of the International Conference on Information Technology and Computer Systems Engineering (ITCSE 2013), Johannesburg, RSA. 27–28, November 2013.*

Rao, U.H. and Nayak, U., (2014). The InfoSec handbook: An introduction to information security. Apress

Ravale, U., Marathe, N., & Padiya, P. (2015). Feature selection based hybrid anomaly intrusion detection system using K means and RBF kernel function. *Procedia Computer Science*, *45*, 428-435.

Rong, C. M., Eggen, S., & Cheng, H. B. (2011). A novel intrusion detection algorithm for wireless sensor networks. In *2nd Int. Conf. on Wireless VITAE* (pp. 1-7). IEEE.

Saeed, A., Ahmadinia, A., Javed, A., & Larijani, H. (2016). Random neural network based intelligent intrusion detection for wireless sensor networks. *Procedia Computer Science*, *80*, 2372-2376.

Sajana, A., Subramanian, R., Kumar, P. V., Krishnan, S., Amrutur, B., Sebastian, J., & Anand, S. V. R. (2009). A low-complexity algorithm for intrusion detection in a pir-based wireless sensor network. In *2009 5th Int. Conf. on ISSNIP* (pp. 337-342). IEEE.

Sajjad, S. M., Bouk, S. H., & Yousaf, M. (2015). Neighbor node trust based intrusion detection system for WSN. *Procedia Computer Science*, *63*, 183-188.

Salehian, S., Masoumiyan, F., & Udzir, N. I. (2010). Energy-Efficient Intrusion Detection in Wireless Sensor Network. *Sensor Networks*, *4*, 207-212.

Sandhya, G., & Julian, A. (2014). Intrusion detection in wireless sensor network using genetic K-means algorithm. In *Int. Conf. on ICACCCT* (pp. 1791-1794). IEEE.

Sarigiannidis, P., Karapistoli, E., & Economides, A. A. (2015). Detecting Sybil attacks in wireless sensor networks using UWB ranging-based information. *Expert Systems with Applications*, *42*(21), 7560-7572.

Sedjelmaci, H., Senouci, S.M. and Feham, M. (2012). Intrusion detection framework of cluster-based wireless sensor network. In *2012 IEEE Symposium on Computers and Communications (ISCC)* (pp. 000893-000897). IEEE

Selvaraj, R., Kuthadi, V. M., & Marwala, T (2016). Ant-based distributed denial of service detection technique using roaming virtual honeypots. *IET Communications*, *10*(8): 929-935. DOI: 10.1049/iet-com.2015.0497.

Selvaraj, R., Kuthadi, V. M., & Marwala, T. (2015). An Effective ODAIDS-HPS Approach for Preventing, Detecting, and Responding to DDoS Attacks. *British Journal of Applied Science & Technology*, *5*(5), 500-509. DOI: 10.9734/BJAST/2015/13386.

Selvaraj, R., Kuthadi, V. M. & Marwala, T. (2014). Enhancing Intrusion Detection system Performance using Firecol Protection Services based honeypot system. *International Journal of Computer Applications, ICCCMIT 2014*, *3*, 43-48.

Selvaraj R., Kuthadi V. M., & Marwala T. (2016). EIDPS: An Efficient Approach to Protect the Network and Intrusion Prevention. In S. Satapathy, J. Mandal, S. Udgata, & V. Bhateja (eds.), *Information Systems Design and Intelligent Applications. Advances in Intelligent Systems and Computing*, vol. 434. New Delhi: Springer. DOI: 10.1007/978-81-322-2752-6_4.

Selvaraj, R., Kuthadi, V. M., & Marwala, T. (2016). Honey Pot: A Major Technique for Intrusion Detection. In *Proceedings of the Second International Conference on Computer and Communication Technologies* (pp. 73-82). New Delhi: Springer. DOI: 10.1007/978-81-322-2523-2_7.

Shamshirband, S., Anuar, N. B., Kiah, M. L. M., & Patel, K. A. (2013). An appraisal and design of a multi-agent system based cooperative wireless intrusion detection computational intelligence technique. *Engineering Applications of Artificial Intelligence*, *26*(9), 2105-2127.

Shamshirband, S., Anuar, N. B., Kiah, M. L. M., Rohani, V. A., Petković, D., Misra, S., & Khan, A. N. (2014). Co-FAIS: cooperative fuzzy artificial immune system for detecting intrusion in wireless sensor networks. *Journal of NCA*, *42*, 102-117.

Shen, S., Li, Y., Xu, H., & Cao, Q. (2011). Signaling game based strategy of intrusion detection in wireless sensor networks. *Computers & Mathematics with Applications*, *62*(6), 2404-2416.

Shih, H. C., Ho, J. H., Liao, B. Y., & Pan, J. S. (2013). Fault node recovery algorithm for a wireless sensor network. *IEEE Sensors Journal*, *13*(7), 2683-2689.

Sokol, P., Husak, M., & Liptak, F. (2013). Deploying Honeypots and Honeynets: Issue of Privacy. *CSN, 4*, 397-403.

Stetsko, A., Folkman, L., & Matyas, V. (2010). Neighbor-based intrusion detection for wireless sensor networks. In *6th Int. Conf. on ICWMC* (pp. 420-425). IEEE.

Su, W. T., Chang, K. M., & Kuo, Y. H. (2007). eHIP: An energy-efficient hybrid intrusion prohibition system for cluster-based wireless sensor networks. *Computer Networks*, *51*(4), 1151-1168.

Subba, B., Biswas, S., & Karmakar, S. (2016). Intrusion detection in Mobile Ad-hoc Networks: Bayesian game formulation. *Engineering Science and Technology: An International Journal*, *19*(2), 782-799.

Sun, B., Shan, X., Wu, K., & Xiao, Y. (2013). Anomaly detection based secure in-network aggregation for wireless sensor networks. *IEEE Systems Journal*, *7*(1), 13-25.

Sun, T., & Liu, X. (2013). Agent-based intrusion detection and self-recovery system for wireless sensor networks. In *5th IEEE Int. Conf. on IC-BNMT* (pp. 206-210). IEEE.

Tian, J., & Gao, M. (2009). Intelligent community intrusion detection system based on wireless sensor network and fuzzy neural network. In *ISECS Int. Colloquium on CCCM*, vol. 3 (pp. 102-105). IEEE.

Tseng, H. W., Lee, Y. H., Yen, L. Y., Yu, S. Y., & Chen, Y. L. (2015). ZigBee (2.4 G) wireless sensor network application on indoor intrusion detection. In *IEEE International Conference on ICCE-TW* (pp. 434-435). IEEE.

Vamsi, P. R., & Kant, K. (2015). Secure data aggregation and intrusion detection in wireless sensor networks. In *2015 Int. Conf. on ICSC* (pp. 127-131). IEEE.

Wang, Y., Fu, W., & Agrawal, D. P. (2013). Gaussian versus uniform distribution for intrusion detection in wireless sensor networks. *IEEE Transactions on Parallel and Distributed systems*, *24*(2), 342-355.

Wang, S. S., Yan, K. Q., Wang, S. C., & Liu, C. W. (2011). An integrated intrusion detection system for cluster-based wireless sensor networks. *Expert Systems with Applications*, *38*(12), 15234-15243.

Wang, Y., Fu, W., & Agrawal, D. P. (2013). Gaussian versus uniform distribution for intrusion detection in wireless sensor networks. *IEEE Transactions on Parallel and Distributed systems*, *24*(2), 342-355.

Wang, C., Ma, H., He, Y., & Xiong, S. (2012). Adaptive approximate data collection for wireless sensor networks. *IEEE Transactions on Parallel and Distributed Systems*, *23*(6), 1004-1016.

Wang, Y., Wang, X., Xie, B., Wang, D., & Agrawal, D. P. (2008). Intrusion detection in homogeneous and heterogeneous wireless sensor networks. *IEEE transactions on mobile computing*, *7*(6), 698-711.

Wu, H.C., (2013). An empirical study of the effects of service quality, perceived value, corporate image, and customer satisfaction on behavioral intentions in the Taiwan quick service restaurant industry. Journal of Quality Assurance in Hospitality & Tourism, 14(4), pp.364-390.

Yan, K. Q., Wang, S. C., Wang, S. S., & Liu, C. W. (2010). Hybrid intrusion detection system for enhancing the security of a cluster-based wireless sensor network. In *3rd IEEE Int. Conf. on ICCSIT*, vol. 1 (pp. 114-118). IEEE.

Yu, Q., Luo, Z., & Min, P. (2010). Intrusion Detection in Wireless Sensor Networks for Destructive Intruders. In *Proceedings of APSIPA Annual Summit and Conference 2015*, *4*, 68-75.

Yu, Z., & Tsai, J. J. (2008). A framework of machine learning based intrusion detection for wireless sensor networks. In *IEEE Int. Conf. on Sensor Networks (SUTC '08)* (pp. 272-279). IEEE.

Zhang, X., He, J., & Wei, Q. (2009). Key Management Integrated with Intrusion Detection in Wireless Sensor Networks. In *Int. Sym. on CNMT 2009* (pp. 1-4). IEEE.

Zhao, J., & Liu, N. (2011). A Dynamic Intrusion Detection Model Based on Immunity for Wireless Sensor Network. In *3rd Int. Workshop on ISA* (pp. 1-3). IEEE.

Zhao, Z., Braun, T., do Rosario, D., Cerqueira, E., Immich, R., & Curado, M. (2012). QoE-aware FEC mechanism for intrusion detection in multi-tier wireless multimedia sensor networks. In *IEEE 8th Int. Conf. on WiMob* (pp. 689-696). IEEE.

Zhijie, H., & Ruchuang, W. (2012). Intrusion detection for wireless sensor network based on traffic prediction model. *Physics Procedia*, *25*, 2072-2080.